Component Design

'NE WEEK LOAN

'003

Before the real city could be seen it had to be imagined

(*In the Skin of the Lion* by Michael Ondaatje, p. 29, 1997, Picador)

Component Design

Michael Stacey

Architectural Press

OXFORD   AUCKLAND   BOSTON   JOHANNESBURG   MELBOURNE   NEW DELHI

An imprint of Butterworth-Heinemann
Linacre House, Jordan Hill, Oxford OX2 8DP
225 Wildwood Avenue, Woburn, MA 01801–2041
A division of Reed Educational and Professional Publishing Ltd

 A member of the Reed Elsevier plc group

First published 2001

© Michael Stacey, 2001

British Library Cataloguing in Publication Data
Stacey, Michael
    Component design
    1. Architectural design   2. Buildings, Prefabricated
    I. Title
    721'.04497

ISBN 0 7506 0913 3

Composition by Scribe Design, Gillingham, Kent, UK
Printed and bound in Italy by Printer Trento S.r.l.

FOR EVERY VOLUME THAT WE PUBLISH, BUTTERWORTH-HEINEMANN
WILL PAY FOR BTCV TO PLANT AND CARE FOR A TREE.

Contents

Acknowledgements

This book would not have been possible without the support and inspiration of Margaret Stacey and Frank Stacey, who sadly died in 1977, and the patience of my children, Frances, Robert and Thomas. The critical input of Cody Gaynor, Chris Grech and Ron Fitch of AME has been invaluable. Thanks also go to Peter Stacey for Y Bwced Perfaith and Deyth Jenkins for Ary Fein.

The illustrations were drawn by Maja Åasted, Ko Ming-Wah and Gary Sutherland with additional picture research by Aradhana Gupta. For formatting and final delivery of the manuscript, thanks go to David Aye and Alison Moore. The cover was designed by André Ikier.

A significant contribution to this book has been made by all who have worked at Brookes Stacey Randall, and in particular Nik Randall. Not forgetting the clients without whom the projects would not come to fruition.

Thanks also go to the many architects, engineers, product designers, specialist sub-contractors and manufacturers who supplied information and photographs.

Colour printing in this book has been sponsored by ⓐ ⓜ ⓔ .

Disclaimer

The information contained in this book has been thoroughly checked. However, not all future developments are positive, companies are taken over and techniques are dropped, sizes are varied and are not always increased. Also new technologies are being invented and developed. Therefore it is the reader's responsibility to check for him or herself. As stated at the beginning of this book, it is intended as a primer, a gateway to further information and not a substitute to direct communication with the many people who make, shape, form, finish and install components.

Foreword

Currently the majority of building envelopes are detailed by the cladding subcontractor and most of the elements are catalogue items. While this approach can result in short-term savings to the client, it can often lead to an impoverished architecture.

'Component Design' is a timely reminder that one of the keys to creating rich and refined architecture lies in understanding the methods of production.

Practitioners may be intimidated by their own lack of experience in attempting to design a component from first principles. Although this is not a book on how to design components it does examine a wide range of production and fabrication methods for a wide range of materials, and provides clues on how to begin. The approach is relevant to any prefabricated structure or product.

One defining aspect of twenthieth century architecture was its engagement with the idea of mass production. The best architecture of that period almost certainly helped to define product lines that we continue to use. As catalogue architecture shows, however, there is a need to continue to foster this close relationship with the making process, in order to encourage change and development without which architecture could be in danger of becoming 'cookie cutter' similar.

Michael Stacey is clearly aware of this situation and is dedicated in his work and writing to encouraging the development of a fruitful collaboration between designers and producers. He also reminds us that if sufficient attention and time are given to this area of practice, one can truly make a silk purse rather than have to put up with a sow's ear.

TIM MACFARLANE
BSc CEng FRSA MIStructE HonFRIBA
Creative Design Partner of Dewhurst Macfarlane and Partners.

Tim Macfarlane is recognized internationally as an innovative structural engineer w'
works closely with architects and clients and has a particular interest in the f'
struct'

ERRATA

A full list of photograph/illustration credits is given below.

Cover picture: Peter Durant/André Ikier/Brookes Stacey Randall; Figure 1.1: Luca Anichini; Figures 1.2, 4.17, 6.1, 6.17: Peter Durant; Figure 1.3: M.F. Ashby; Figure 1.4: James Morris; Figures 1.5a, 1.5b: Peter Keetman; Figure 1.6, 6.6: Ken Kirkwood; Figure 1.7: Audi; Figure 1.8: Peter Cook; Figure 1.9: Ron Arad Associates; Figure 1.10: James Dyson; Figure 2.1: James Linden; Figures 2.2b, 2.8, 2.11, 2.17, 2.18, 2.19, 3.8, 3.14, 3.25, 5.17, 5.18, 6.32, 6.33, 7.2, 7.3, 7.8, 7.9, 7.11, 7.14: Brookes Stacey Randall; Figure 2.2c: MAG; Figures 2.2a, 2.3, 2.4, 2.33, 2.35, 2.42, 3.3, 3.9, 4.6, 4.9, 4.10, 4.16, 5.8, 5.12, 5.13, 5.14, 5.15, 6.5, 6.13, 6.19, 6.20: Michael Stacey; Figure 2.5: Richard Rogers and Partners; Figures 2.6, 3.15: John Linden; Figures 2.7, 2.30, 4.1, 4.4, 4.13, 4.28, 4.29, 6.34, 6.35: Richard Davies; Figure 2.9: Corus; Figure 2.10: Nik Randall; Figures 2.12, 2.13: Richard Horden; Figures 2.14, 3.17: Ian Lambot/Watermark Publications; Figure 2.15: Viaduct; Figure 2.16: DRL/Michael Stacey; Figure 2.20: NASA; Figure 2.21: Jo Reid and John Peck; Figures 2.22, 5.4: Jean Prouvé; Figure 2.23: Presslock, Corus, Stoakes Systems; Figures 2.24, 2.25, 4.27: Foster & Partners; Figures 2.26, 2.27, 2.28: Festo Corporate Design; Figure 2.29: RAHU; Figures 2.31, 2.32, 4.8, 4.11, 4.14, 5.10: **ame**; Figure 2.34: Sika; Figures 2.36, 2.37, 2.38: Neil Burford; Figure 2.39: Marcon Limited/Osborn Steel Extrusions Limited; Figure 2.40: Osborn Steel Extrusions Limited; Figure 2.41: Department of the Environment; Figures 3.1, 3.4, 3.10: Sheffield Forgemasters; Figure 3.2: Dr Nieswagg/Michael Stacey; Figure 3.5: Ove Arup & Partners; Figures 3.6, 3.7: RFR; Figure 3.11: Michael Stacey and Chris Grech; Figures 3.12, 3.13: MBC; Figure 3.16: Cupples; Figures 3.18, 4.20: Michael Hopkins & Partners; Figure 3.19: Waddington Galleries; Figure 3.20: CYMAT Corporation; Figure 3.21: Price & Myers; Figures 3.22, 3.23: Peter Strobel; Figure 3.24: Nicholas Grimshaw & Partners; Figure 3.26: IAA - Brookes Stacey Randall; Figure 4.2: Kingspan; Figure 4.3: BDP; Figure 4.5: Superform; Figure 4.7: Christian Smith, **ame**; Figure 4.12: Majors; Figure 4.15: Erika Barahona Ede; Figures 4.18, 4.19: Richard Bryant/ARCAID; Figure 4.21: Superform; Figures 4.22, 4.23, 4.24, 4.25, 4.26: Superform/Michael Stacey; Figure 5.1: Professor Paul Smith; Figure 5.2: Corus; Figure 5.3: British Aerospace; Figure 5.5: Hunter Douglas Construction Elements; Figures 5.6, 5.7, 7.13: Danish Design Council; Figure 5.9: Coseley Panel Systems; Figures 5.11, 5.16: Advanced Composites; Figure 6.2: Robert Nissje/Michael Stacey; Figures 6.3, 6.8, 6.9, 6.18: Pilkington; Figure 6.4: Graydon Wood 1992; Figure 6.7: Groupe ALTO; Figure 6.10: Galia Amsel; Figure 6.11: National Glass Centre; Figure 6.12: Deide Von Schawen; Figure 6.14: GGF/Michael Stacey; Figure 6.15: Stoakes Systems; Figure 6.16: Saint Gobain-Solaglas; Figures 6.21, 6.22, 6.25: ABT; Figure 6.23: Chris Gascoigne; Figure 6.24: Dennis Gilbert; Figure 6.26: Andrew Putler; Figure 6.27: Dewhurst Macfarlane; Figures 6.28, 6.29: Kenji Kobayashi; Figure 6.30: Thomas Heatherwick; Figure 6.31: Richard Bryant; Figure 7.1: Michel Denance/Archipress; Figures 7.4, 7.6: BRE; Figures 7.5, 7.10: Taywood Engineering; Figure 7.7: Felix Candela; Figure 7.12: Sandberg Consulting Engineers; Figure 7.15: Dyson; Figure 7.16: Alloy; Figure 7.17a, Paul Ratigan; Figures 7.17b, 7.17c: Elliot Wood Partnership; Figure 7.18: Classic & Sports Car; Figure 7.19: Brookes Stacey Randall/Frost/Melon

Table 2.3: Courtesy of BSI

Frank Gery should read Frank Gehry on Pages 97, 183 and 201, and I.M. Pie should read I.M. Pei on Pages 144, 145 and 204

Page 153: The first three sentences of the final paragraph on this page should read: There is now a range of countersunk fittings that can be specified. Some were developed for specific projects, such as the fitting developed for Parc de la Villette by Rice Francis Ritchie, which was then marketed SIV. Some fittings are direct commercial rivals of Planar and this includes Greenburg Hansen (see Figure 6.19).

1

Introduction

This book is intended to encourage discussion between architects, engineers, designers and manufacturers, and is not a substitute for direct communication. It is a guide to stimulate understanding of the potential of materials and manufacturing processes. Arguably technological development has left a designer spoilt for choice. Are designers bewildered by this diversity? Philip Ball (1997) asks:

> "You want to make an engine part? A vacuum cleaner? A coat hanger? Take your pick – at a rough count, you have between 40 000 and 80 000 materials to chose from. How do you cope with that?"

This book explores specific design constraints, describes processes, and discusses materials including standards and finishes were appropriate. The aim is to inform the value judgements made in the design process. However, it is not encyclopaedic, but more an illustration of an approach, presented in a readable and user-friendly way.

Figure 1.1 Sienna from the Tower del Mangia (photograph by Luca Anichini).

Problem solving has been presented as a model of the design process in architecture as if analysis of programme, site, context, precedent and the available means of construction are sufficient in themselves. Creativity and the intuitive leap, however, are essential. Design is more clearly defined as a continuous and reiterative process of value judgements. Each architect generates their own criteria and aims within the social and economic context of their work, which may well vary greatly with each project, responding not only to the brief but to the contribution of the client and the design team. Within this process of construction one creates problems, often they are 'solved' as they arise by circumvention.

When debating how architecture should develop, there is always a tendency to dogmatically reject the values other designers have brought to their work. It is more important to establish the criteria for a particular project and follow this through rigorously within its own intellectual framework. For this author, architecture is more akin to the creation of a work of literature than of reductive problem solving. Design is in essence a delta of opportunity, an exploration of the possible. The art and craft of architecture should throw off the remnants of scientific reductivism much as science has itself. For Peter Zumthor (1998).

Figure 1.2 Thames Water Tower (architect Brookes Stacey Randall).

"construction is the art of making a meaningful whole out of many parts. Buildings are witnesses to the human ability to construct concrete things. I believe the real core of all architectural work lies in the art of construction. At a point in time when concrete materials are assembled and erected, the architecture we have been looking for becomes part of the real world. I feel respect for the art of joining, the ability of craftsmen and engineers. I am impressed by man's knowledge of how to make things. . ."

This book is the by-product of 20 years experience in designing component-based architecture. It is in essence the book I looked for and could not find when at

Liverpool University School of Architecture. The technological potential of society appeared to be increasing dramatically but the sources of information were fragmented and sometimes obtuse. The opportunities created, and the combination of finite constraints and almost infinite possibilities fascinated me. The potential to extend the possible by probing, logic and the intuitive leap inherent in design.

Having worked on the Hong Kong and Shanghai Bank and the Renault Centre with Norman Foster and colleagues, I qualified as an architect whilst designing composite metal panels systems for RVP Building Products Ltd., now **ame**. This experience has widened since I founded Brookes Stacey Randall in 1987. Much of the book is like a 'surgeon's report' based directly on project and consultancy

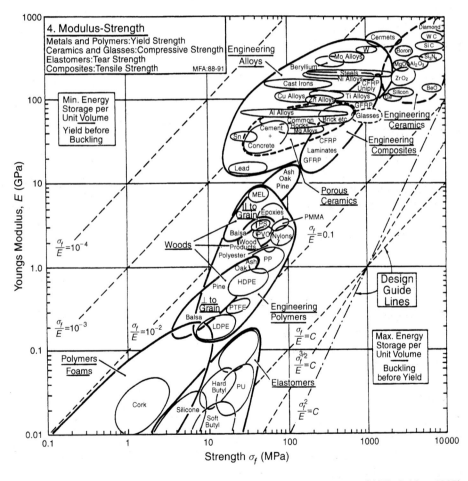

Figure 1.3 Young's Modulus plotted against strength (chart courtesy of M.F. Ashby, 1987).

experience and is a result of direct dialogue with manufacturers and specialist suppliers. The widest possible range of examples is included from the work of many inspirational architects, product designers and engineers, within the scope of each chapter. The book is part of a personal commitment to life-long learning and the dissemination of ideas.

There are surprisingly few books that seek to explore the relationship between the overall intention of a project and the means of achieving it. The relationship between ideas and details, junctions and spaces are seldom thoroughly discussed. A valid criticism of some of the architects of the Modern Movement is that in promoting the social art of architecture they lost touch with the direct art of architecture. Ford (1990) suggests in his book that 'detailing was born when craftsmanship died' and it is evident that construction has been compartmentalized. The design team is now divided into groups of consultants each representing one part of the whole, generating individual disciplines and divided interests. Similarly the contractor, whatever the form of contract, does not build the work. He marshals a team of subcontractors. Ford suggests that this process of specialization has a greater importance to the method of construction than prefabrication.

The end of craftsmanship has been predicted many times in the last two centuries. To achieve excellence in architecture it has to be re-invented. Frank Lloyd Wright in his lecture 'The Art and Craft of the Machine' at Hull House in 1901 stated that machines should not be used to produce miles of meaningless moulding. He had invited several of his subcontractors in the hope that they 'would tell us what we might do to help them'. It is essential to access centres of specialist knowledge and to source areas of new skills in material science and construction. Batch production and prefabrication is an appropriate yet exacting route to high constructional quality. As Chris Wilkinson (1991; p. vii) states:

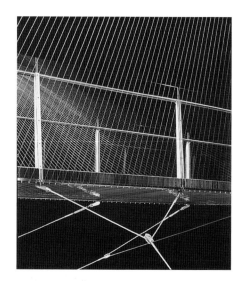

Figure 1.4 Active steel and glass bridge in the Challenge of Materials Gallery at Science Museum, London (architect Wilkinson Eyre with Bryn Bird of Engineer, Whitby and Bird).

"There is a kind of architecture which is not formal, decorated or mannered, but derives its aesthetic from a clear expression of its purpose and component parts, where the demands of function and economy have led to simplicity of form and construction but where the basic requirements of enclosure and structure are extended by design to create buildings of quality."

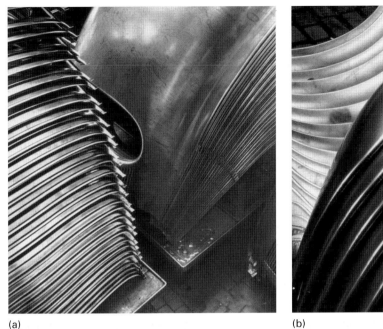

(a)   (b)

Figure 1.5 (a) Pressed steel Beetle roofs and (b) pressed steel Beetle rear wings (photographs by Peter Keetman).

The issues raised by Ruskin and Morris of man's relationship to the machine and mass production was a fundamental theme of the twentieth century, and remains a challenge to the art and architecture of the twenty-first century. On one side, mankind's ability to repeatedly make reliable products and the advances of constructional technologies such as suspended glazing, allows us to achieve the new forms of construction that the Modern Movement dreamed of, and to present new opportunities to the building's user; a humane architecture first and foremost. On the other side, the layering and copying of materials challenges the onlooker to identify the true material from the copy. Honesty, always a difficult concept in architecture, has never been more tested.

Technology transfer

In each chapter a brief history of technological development is included to fuel understanding of a particular technique and to trace the time frame from 'Blue Sky' research to robust and reliable building components. Clearly the construction industry can learn from other fields, benefiting in part from much higher

R&D expenditure. The extent to which construction can learn from its own best practice is often understated and overlooked, as Isaac Newton wrote in a letter to Robert Hooke: 'If I have seen further it is because I am standing on the shoulders of giants'. However, it is vital to remember that Newton was one of the most original thinkers of the age of enlightenment and as the Finnish architect, Eliel Saarinen stated, 'you cannot live on the half digested food of others'.

The concept of technology transfer was launched by Martin Pawley in the Architectural Review, September 1987, using the imagery of Richard Horden's Yacht House with its extruded aluminium structure. Indeed, the design of trains, boats and aerospace R&D is stimulating development in the use of aluminium. The emphasis on fuel efficiency, safety and recyclability is leading to an increased use of aluminium in car design. The Audi A8 makes extensive use of aluminium and was designed to meet 1997 US safety standards. It is built around an aluminium space frame and is probably the first generally successful aluminium space frame. This space frame with its curvilinear geometry and complex junctions is formed of extruded sections jointed with vacuum cast nodes. The development process including the testing of new alloys took 10 years.

Figure 1.6 Yacht House by Richard Horden Associates.

The case for technology transfer should not be overstated; the production of an aluminium extrusion for a building component is identical for a car, a yacht or a chair. The technology is not transferred, the source is the same extrusion plants, which is readily accessible to all designers. The relative economy of a new extrusion die

Figure 1.7 Space frame of Audi 8.

means that to produce a purpose-made extrusion does not require a multimillion-pound R&D budget.

Robust technologies

One of the problems facing architects today is a lack of reliable or robust constructional technology, especially when materials and techniques from diverse backgrounds are used in conjunction. Steven Groak (1992; p. 180) states that 'One implication is that all building projects will have to be treated as innovative'. This has lead to the development of the 'practitioner–researcher', one of the primary engines of R&D in construction. Leading practices use each building as a vehicle to learn and to develop, and to innovate when appropriate. Composite cladding, which is discussed in Chapter 5, is cited by Steven Groak as a prime example of a successful development process, lead by architects and with little or no declared R&D budget.

Dimensional co-ordination or the tyranny of a grid

There is a tendency to always bracket prefabrication with 'dimensional co-ordination', modularity and grids. This at times in the twentieth century has lead to sterility in architecture. If a planning grid is used as a tyrannical ordering device it potentially results in three problems.

• The actual materials and their thicknesses are ignored or suppressed.
• The details are wasteful in materials and or structural components.
• The resultant geometry of the building does not respond to the needs of the occupants, and is based on a crude understanding of production techniques.

This no longer needs to be the case. But did it ever? The building grid should be a design tool not a tyrannical preconception of how elements are made and how they can be made economically. The geometry of the spaces should be determined by the architect, the intended use, and the desired aesthetic (Muranka and Rootes, 1996). Particularly in housing, the author believes that it is essential that the design, even if totally prefabricated, does not suggest to the viewer or occupant that mechanization has taken command (Giedion, 1948).

The Camellia House at Wollaton Hall, Nottingham 'may be one of the earliest examples of a completely prefabricated iron building' (Koppelkamm, 1981). However, it is not an example of modular production, but was manufactured as a one-off design by Jones & Clark of Birmingham in 1823. There is no record of the involvement of an architect, and Gilbert Herbert suggests that it was either Jeffrey Wyatville or C.R. Cockerell. Stefan Koppelkamm suggests it may have been designed by Jones & Clark using Cockerell's earlier Camellia House at The Grange, Hampshire as a precedent. In this context it is significant as a building which uses repetitive cast components. The building, however, was conceived for the particular need of camellias and has an irregular, polygonal ground plan partly resulting from being built against the wall of an existing higher terrace.

Modularity can be used as a conceptual approach, as in contemporary car production, where the module is a conceptual ordering device and not a spatial straitjacket. Modular steel partitions, as produced by Hauseman or Unilock, became an embodiment of Conrad Wachsmann's tartan grid. However, they have limited spanning capabilities and the junctions or capping pieces have to be identical to the partition thickness or full modularity does not result. Most partition manufacturers went on to develop fine line junctions to offer a different expression or to incorporate other components such as shelving or services. There are many examples of gasketed cladding systems proposed by Richard Rogers, Nicholas Grimshaw and others, which seek to continue and fulfil this modular approach. Often the geometrical problems encountered were simplified by the use of extruded building forms, such as in the Sainsbury Centre at the University of East Anglia (UEA) by Foster or the Patera system by Michael Hopkins. In each case the end wall is treated as the non-standard condition, thus greatly simplifying the panel geometry. Panel clad buildings often show more geometrical similarity to a Renaissance courtyard than to the work of Wachsmann (1961), responding to the challenge of taking a regular rhythm around a corner.

Geometry

It is essential to understand and communicate the geometry of the component and building assembly. The use of computers in the design process has stimulated interest and confidence in creating buildings using non-linear geometries. Towards the end of the twentieth century there were examples of projects which were unnecessarily complex formally, which impoverished their realization. The geometric complexity of the detailing was greater than the contractor or possible budget could withstand. Perhaps for some the close inspection of their buildings may not concern them!

Prototypes and testing

The vital role of samples, prototypes and testing in innovation is discussed in the final chapter alongside the motivation behind innovation. The confidence gained from physical testing cannot be overstated.

Design for manufacture

There is an increasing understanding of the need to design for manufacture, to design components and assemblies that can be produced rather than being conceived first and then redesigned in order to be manufactured. This goes beyond issues of buildablity and requires the designer to gain detailed understanding of the manufacturing process. This has been characterized as lean production or lean thinking. However, adopting the principle of designing for manufacture does not imply a conservative approach. The boundaries of the possible should be explored and extended. Design for manufacture, particularly when used in conjunction with rapid prototyping techniques, can very significantly reduce lead-time and increase cost effectiveness. Existing sub-assemblies are increasingly being redesigned as single components, which embody all the functional and geometrical needs of the earlier assembly, often with the added benefit of short production times.

This book therefore seeks to forge a link between design and manufacture. Many of the examples illustrated in this text harness industrial processes, resulting in

Figure 1.8
Waterloo
International
(architect
Nicholas
Grimshaw and
Partners, engineer
Anthony Hunt
Associates).

affordable components of fine tolerance and high quality of finish. There is an emphasis on processes that result in elements that are fully three-dimensional. Linear and sheet components are included but these are shown in the context of their three-dimensional use.

Tolerance

All components and the materials they are made from vary. A tolerance is a permitted variation in any characteristic: dimension, weight or formulation etc. Too often in construction, tolerances are not clearly understood and are used as an excuse for poorly executed work. To construct a building successfully one of the key tasks is to define the tolerance range of the component and the materials to be used and to work to these. This does not mean that all elements need to be to fine tolerances. It is the agreed deviation that is critical; if too fine tolerances are required the components will become unnecessarily expensive.

Dimensional tolerances can be classified as:

• manufacturing tolerances, i.e. the accuracy with which a sheet of glass can be cut

- assembly tolerances, i.e. the combination of the tolerances of a number of components
- site work tolerance, i.e. the accuracy with which a shutter for reinforced concrete can be made.

It is not advisable just to work to the tolerances stated in the British Standard or Euro Norm as these can prove to be too high a degree of variation for one's specific needs. Often manufacturers can and will expect to work to tighter tolerances if asked. The key is to ask and to define the requirements clearly, typically in a specification.

Tolerances are often confused with other sources of variation in construction, in particular thermal movement or movement resulting from variation in moisture content. In designing a glazing system to fit to a long span steel structure, such as the East Croydon Station with its 55 metre span, it was necessary to accommodate geometrical variation, thermal movement and deflections resulting from loading. During the construction process it was necessary to measure the rise and fall of the steel work with the diurnal temperature range so that this could be excluded from the erection tolerances and the agreed range achieved. It is important with some components to consider negative as well as positive thermal movement; this is noted in the European Standard for composite panels. The thermal coefficients for many of the materials mentioned in this book are given at the start of each chapter and in table form in book's website.

At times tolerances are portrayed as just a visual problem! However, lack of fit can lead to the premature failure of a component and to future problems such as leaking. How did the visual criteria for a building or its components become separated from the other criteria of judgement during the twentieth century? The visual criteria may to an extent be a subjective area, but it is as important a set of criteria as any physical parameter that can be defined. For many materials non-subjective visual comparitives are available and incorporating a sample inspection process into the procurement process is very beneficial and time well spent; disputes can be minimized at an early stage rather than at a latter and often more costly stage of the construction process.

Part of the challenge is the accuracy of the human eye, which can judge difference or acuity to 1000th of an inch or 0.0254 mm. For example, the human eye is used by Nissan to check colour match between car body components. It is revealing that the famous nineteenth century mechanical engineer Sir Joseph Whitworth, who is accredited with the production of 'the true plane' surface and became the first person to measure the difference of one millionth of an inch or 2.54×10^{-5} mm, also founded the Whitworth Art Gallery in Manchester.

James Dyson stated that 'Industry, manufacturing is a creative act' (Gow, 1998); in essence it exists for you to interact with. Manufacturers are transforming their activity into a service industry where the physical output is tailored directly to meet their clients needs.

Figure 1.9 Boop low table by Ron Arad produced using cavity-formed superplastic aluminium.

References

Ashby, M.F. (1987). *Materials Selection in Mechanical Design*, Pergamon Press.

Ball, P. (1997). *Made to Measure*, p. 9. Princeton University Press.

Ford, E.R. (1990). *The Details of Modern Architecture*, Vol. 1. MIT Press p. 7.

Giedion, S. (1948). *Mechanization Takes Command*. Oxford University Press.

Gow, D. (1998). Interview with James Dyson. *The Guardian*, 5 September.

Groak, S. (1992). *The Idea of Building*. E&FN Spon.

Koppelkamm, S. (1981). *Glasshouses and Wintergardens of the Nineteenth Century*. Granada.

Muranka, T. and Rootes, N. (1996). "doing a dyson". Dyson Appliances Limited.

Wachsmann, C. (1961). *Turning Point of Building Structure and Design*. Reinhold.

Wilkinson, C. (1991). *Supersheds*. Butterworth Architecture.

Zumthor, P., Achleitner, F., Nakao, H. (1998). *Architecture and Urbanism*. February, extra edition, A U Publishing, Japan, ISBN 4-900211-5-8.

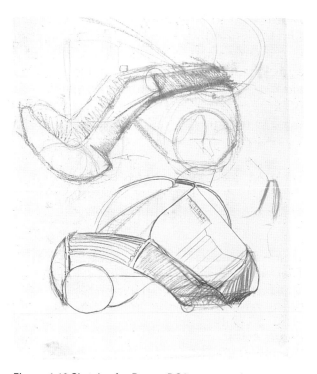

Figure 1.10 Sketch of a Dyson DO2 vacuum cleaner.

2

Extrusions

2.1 Aluminium Extrusions

Aluminium is one of the many materials available to designers to realize their intentions. Evaluated against other material it might be selected for its durability, its adaptability and its relative economy. Interest in this material may be characterized by its visual and tactile qualities, the precision of its manufacture, and the diversity of possible finishes.

Aluminium in itself has remained unchanged since it was discovered in 1807 by Sir Humphry Davy and H. C. Oersted first produced it in 1855. However, aluminium is primarily used in alloys. The alloys for many architectural applications use the addition of magnesium and silicon to improve the mechanical properties of the aluminium. The commonly available alloys are classified in BS EN 485 and BS EN 755 and have very well defined performance characteristics. The internationally recognized four-figure code used to describe aluminium alloys defines the

Table 2.1 Material properties of aluminium

Property	Value
Density	2720 kg/m^3
Young's modulus	70 kN/mm^2
Thermal conductivity	237 W/m°C
Coefficient of thermal expansion	2.3 × 10^{-5}/°C
Corrosion resistance	Excellent
Melting point	660°C
Recyclability	Excellent
Primary embodied energy*	544 GJ/m^3

*Data supplied by BRE

Figure 2.1 Entrance to East Croydon station (architect Brookes Stacey Randall).

content of the alloy. The application of aluminium in construction and even the material itself continues to be developed as new technical discoveries are made and exploited. The development of new alloys can offer increased performance. Seco Aluminium in the late 1990s developed a new alloy based on 6082 but with a greater ductility. Seco were seeking to produce a faster running alloy, which would be more economical to produce, by investigating an alloy first produced in 1952. The alloy produced proved to be fast running and strong yet with improved ductility and a 15% elongation; a very formable alloy. This alloy is used for ballistic resistant cladding, exploiting both its strength and its ability to yield.

The aluminium extrusion process enables architects, engineers and designers to have special sections made to their exact requirements at surprisingly low cost. It is also a very direct process, allowing close control over the quality of the product. This chapter is intended as source of guidance for designers who may be considering aluminium extrusions as a component of their buildings or product assemblies.

There are four distinct routes whereby aluminium extrusions can become part of a building:

- as part of a system, e.g. curtain walling
- from stockholders' stock lengths, e.g. standard sections such as T-bars, round tube, Zs and box sections (dimensions still in imperial!)
- from extruders' stock dies, e.g. mouldings, flashings, trims and edgings
- from specially designed custom dies, e.g. for special sections for a particular design.

Proprietary systems: most manufactures would consider altering their system for special projects but only where the installed value of the contract is substantial, that is, say over £250 000. The key is the weight of aluminium required and the complexity of the new section.

Stock lengths: one disadvantage of using stock items is that there is a limited range of sections and a traditional dependence on existing imperial dimensions. This often makes them incompatible with close tolerance metric assembly.

Stock dies: all extruders will produce aluminium sections from their range of stock dies, which are the copyright of the extruder, not its customer.

Although a wider range of sections is obtainable than from stockholders, the only real advantage of stock dies over custom designed dies is that the die exists. This therefore eliminates the drawing approval period, die cutting and associated costs, thus reducing the time from the order to the availability of the section.

Custom dies: there are at least twenty companies in the UK that can provide aluminium extrusions to customers' orders. Companies such as Allusuisse, Hydro Aluminium, Kaye, Sapa or Nedal will provide special extrusions to order, a typical timescale is 6 weeks to approve the sample and a further 4 weeks for production. The steel dies required to extrude a given shape are relatively inexpensive, the cost being related to the size and complexity of the section (see below).

The use of computer-aided design (CAD) and related software has speeded the production of custom dies. Extruders offer a prompt service, producing die drawings including sectional strength characteristics, weight and surface area. This software is available for architects and engineers to use directly in the design process.

Extrusion process

Cylindrical or elliptical billets of aluminium, weighing up to 200 kg, are first heated to a temperature of around 500°C before being placed in a steel container and forced, while still in a hot plastic state,

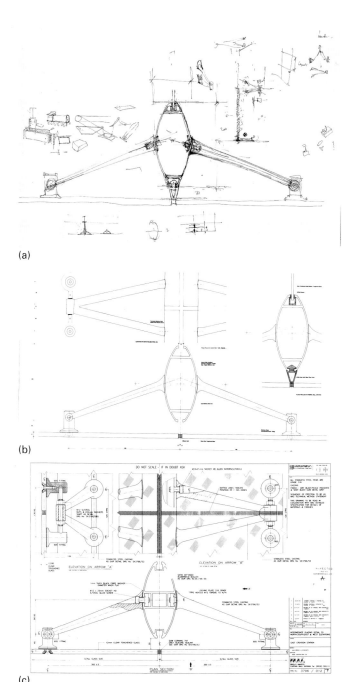

(a)

(b)

(c)

Figure 2.2 (a) East Croydon mullion (author's initial sketch). (b) Brookes Stacey Randall's tender drawing. (c) MAG's inspected shop drawing.

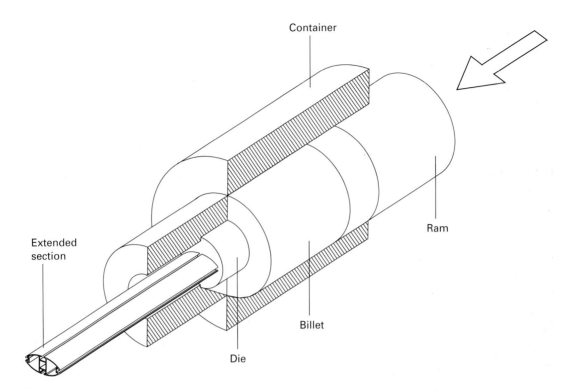

Figure 2.3 Diagram of an extrusion press.

through a steel die by a hydraulic ram to form the extrusion. The shape of the resulting section is governed by the die and by the ram forces applied. By using pre-heated billets and an autoloader, the hydraulic press can produce a continuous extrusion, the force of the ram being sufficient to weld the front of the new billet to the rear of the old as they are forced through.

The emerging section is air cooled and guided down a run-out table of rollers before being automatically cut into production lengths of up to 40 metres. This is governed by the length of the table. A controlled stretch is then applied to each length to straighten it before being cut to order. The length may have to be oversized to allow for anodizing or other finishing processes.

The process is rapid. A hydraulic press can extrude at rates in excess of 20 m/min, depending upon the size and shape of the section. For heat treatable alloys the process is completed by a precipitation or ageing treatment, the extruded length being baked in an oven at 175°C for 5–15 hours.

The size of an extrusion is dependent on the size and ram pressure of the press; predominately circular die chambers and cylindrical billets of aluminium are used. The size of the die is therefore determined by the circumscribing diameter (CCD), which is defined as the minimum diameter that the extrusion can be contained within. Hydraulic presses are described by their ram pressure and by the maximum size extrusion that can be produced (see Table 2.2). The maximum

Table 2.2

	Max. Ram Pressure (Tonnes)	Max. Extrusion Size (circumscribing circle diameter in millimetres)
Alusuisse UK	10,000	600 (elongated shapes 800 × 100)
Nedal	4000	410
Reynolds	3500	400
Alcoa (Swansea)	3150	270
Aluminium Shapes Boal UK	140	
Alcoa (Banbury)	2000	210
British Aluminium Speciality Extrusions (high strength alloys only)	5000	360
British Aluminium Tubes	600	100
	3000/4000 seamless tubes	160
	5000 seamless tubes	280
(Tubes only) Capital	600 (indirect)	72
Hydro Aluminium	1600	150
	2200	190
	3200	200
Kaye Aluminium	2000	195
Sapa – Tibshelf	2800	200 (elongated shapes 250 × 70)
Sapa (Cheltenham) (formerly Indalex)	3300	208
Seco Aluminium	1800/1650	165
British Alcan	2750	240
Alcan High Duty	5000	400
Almatex	3000	240

size of extrusion section is therefore governed by the combination of the maximum ram pressure and the size of the die that the press can accommodate. The common size within the UK is a 178 mm or 7 inch press, which leads to a maximum size of 168 mm to allow for the structural stability of the steel die. Extrusion of up to 400 mm can be produced in the UK. Alusuisse have developed a press with a wider slot, like an Underground sign, which enables it to extrude sections up to 600 mm in diameter or 800 mm wide, but only 100 mm high. This was first developed for the floor pan of the German high-speed ICE train. Often the constraint of the size of the die can be overcome by a design that enables a number of extrusions to form the overall component.

Very small extrusions are usually produced by the 'indirect method' where the billet is held firm and the die is pressed into the softened aluminium. For very small extrusions the cost per kilo becomes disproportionately higher due to the tight tolerances required, the care needed in their production, and the fine detail of the die. Applications for very small extrusions in building construction are rare.

Extrusion presses are expensive pieces of capital equipment; however, the steel dies are relatively inexpensive. The relative economy of a new extrusion die means that to produce a purpose-made extrusion does not require a multimillion-pound R&D budget. The cost of a new die is dependent on size and complexity: a die for an extrusion without voids, which could fit within a diameter of 170 mm, can cost £500–700. A hollow die of a similar size can cost £1500–2000. The cost of the extruded section is related to the weight of aluminium used measured in kilograms, and is influenced by the complexities of the section such as the number of enclosed voids. Secondary processes, for example resin milled out thermal breaks, are available directly from the extruder but add to the sectional cost.

The die cost of specially made extrusions, then, is rarely a significant proportion of the extrusion cost where typical commercial quantities are ordered. The cost of extruded metal per kg is influenced by: dimensions and configuration of the section, metal thickness, alloy, speed at which it can be extruded, tolerance limits, and required surface finish.

Extrusion costs per kilogram are lowest for solid shapes and highest for complex hollow shapes, so every effort should be made to obtain the desired structural result with extrusions that are as simple as practicable. A fully enclosed void requires a mandrel or plug in the die, and a semi-hollow shape requires a strong tongue in the die. Both of these must be strongly supported so that the die will withstand extrusion pressure clear to the tip of the tongue. Such features add to the die cost and usually reduce extrusion speed. Often only a slight change in shape converts it to a less expensive classification, yet without compromising its function or appearance. To obtain a good extrusion, the designer will benefit from observing certain principles and early dialogue with the extruder.

Design features

The extrusion process can enable specially designed shapes to be produced at relatively low cost. But to obtain a good extrusion reasonably cheaply the designer has to observe certain principles. These are listed below.

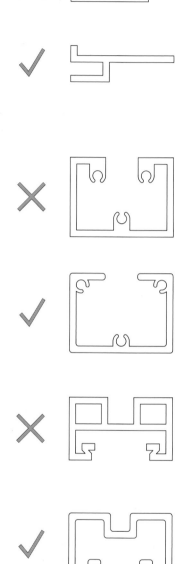

- **Extrusion factor.** The thinner the section, the greater the likelihood of distortion during extrusion. Check the ratio between the circumscribing circle diameter (CCD) and the section thickness.
- **Thickness uniformity.** The metal thickness throughout the extrusion should be as uniform as possible. Where changes are required, for example to increase the strength of a section at a particular part of the extrusion, these changes should be as gradual as possible.
- **Symmetry.** The section of the extrusion should be as symmetrical as possible to reduce the effect of the section twisting as it leaves the die, but like many rules this is often broken at a cost.
- **Open to hollow.** Open sections with open voids, such as a C-shape, are produced using a mandrel or plug in the die. These are generally easier to extrude then sections with enclosed voids, which are produced using a series of bridge dies.
- **Corners.** Corners should be curved where possible. A minimum radius of 0.5 mm is commonly used, which is still visually crisp. Internal corners are governed by the need to produce a readily extruded section or the fit of mating components.
- **Grooves.** Avoid deep narrow slots as much as possible. A good aspect ratio is 3:1.

Figure 2.4 Design features: grooves, screw grooves and minimizing voids.

- One section or two. It can be easier to design a component as two interlocking extruded sections rather than one single section.
- **Finish and tolerance.** The designer needs to identify the critical faces of the extrusion. Tolerances are laid down in BS 1474 and BSEN 755 provides permissible deviations on thickness, length, straightness, and angular and sectional dimensions.

There is general agreement within the industry that the size of die, area balance, and section thickness affect the economics of an extrusion. The speed with which an extrusion can be produced will effect its price per kilogram.

Size of die

The size of the die is determined by the circumscribing circle diameter, which is the minimum diameter of the circle within which the section of extrusion may be contained. In order to keep an unbroken structural ring around the die, the CCD is usually at least 40 mm less than the internal diameter of the billet container or a minimum of 5 mm from the edge of the die. Both die cost and minimum allowable wall thickness increase as the CCD increases.

Area balance

As far as possible the cross section of the extrusion should be distributed equally around the centre of the CCD. In any extrusion, metal flow is slower towards the outside of the die so that by placing thicker parts of the section near the periphery a more even flow of metal is obtained. A well-balanced cross section aids extrusion because it reduces cross flow of metal on the billet side of the die, so the extrusion speed may be higher. Properly designed unbalanced shapes, however, are usually readily extrudable, but at slower speeds and higher costs.

Thickness of metal is probably one of the most important factors governing extrudability and is more complex than simply quoting a fraction of CCD, which is often used as a method of estimating thickness. Section thickness affects extrudability both by its actual and relative position on the die. Small positioning lugs are not considered as having a significant affect on thickness, but excessively thin details and thin ends of elements should be avoided. Thick–thin junctions should also be avoided, but if required should be cornered by rounding or the use of fillets. Even a 0.5-mm radius improves the metal flow compared with a sharp corner. Compared with a cold rolled or hot rolled steel section these radii are not perceptibly rounded.

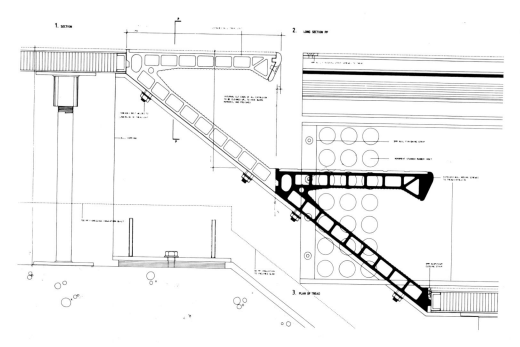

Figure 2.5 Stair tread of Lloyds of London.

However, as with all areas of human invention the above are only guidelines and an extruder can produce sections which bend the rules or even redefine what is possible. The stair tread of Lloyds of London is a perfect example. The general rule is to minimize or avoid the use of voids, but this single extruded tread produced by Nedal in Holland has multiple voids. Apparently the inspiration for this design was John Young of Richard Rogers and Partners seeing a stack of rectangular extrusions in Joseph Gartners' works. The stair tread section can now be seen in the Science Museum, London, as an exemplar of the use of the extrusion process.

Tolerances

Tolerances on the extrusion may also be critical. These are laid down in BS 1474 and BSEN 755. Tolerances are also given for radii of corners, width across flats or hollow sections, and twists of extruded solid or hollow sections or open ends of channels and I-beams. Most manufacturers would reckon to achieve two-thirds of the tolerance levels given in the British Standard. Typical tolerances on aluminium section are shown in Table 2.3.

Table 2.3 Tolerances in BS 1474 for aluminium extrusions

Thickness long	± 0.34 mm	For bars and sections 6–10 m
Length (not applicable to off-line cutting)	± 3.5 mm	For sections circumscribing circle diameter (CCD) over 60 mm diameter and 1.5 m long
Straightness	± 1.55 mm per 1 m	For CCD up to 100 mm
Angular	± 1/2° per 300 mm run	For CCD up to 80 mm
Section dimensions	± 0.65 mm	For widths 80–100 mm

Alloys

Different alloys of aluminium are available for various purposes depending upon performance criteria required, such as strength, durability or conductivity. A complete description of the various alloys and their properties, *The Properties of Aluminium and its Alloys* (2000), is available from the Aluminium Federation. It is the proportion of other metals and elements, such as magnesium and silicon, which modify the performance of the resulting alloy varying from the 6000 series used in curtain walling sections, to the high strength 7000 series, known as aerospace grades. The 7000 series alloys are increasingly being used in bicycle manufacture, and the exclusive association with aerospace is diminishing as other relevant lightweight applications are found.

The previous British Standard coding of these alloys, such as HE30 or HE9, has now been superseded by the 'International Alloy Designations and Chemical Composition Limits for Wrought Aluminum and Wrought Aluminum Alloys' (issued by the Aluminum Association of the USA in July 1998), a four-digit system in which the first digit, which runs from 1 to 9, indicates the principal alloying element. Series 1, 3, 5 and 6 are normally related to products for the building industry. Series 5 (magnesium) is used for sheet products. Series 6 (magnesium/silicone) is used for extruded products.

Thus HE9, which anodizes well and is the most commonly used alloy, becomes 6063 and HE30, which has two-thirds the tensile strength of steel, becomes 6082. This alloy has variable grain structure, which can show throughout the surface of the metal after anodizing. If appearance is critical, it may be necessary to brighten the section by manual or electrolytic polishing before anodizing.

Casting alloys are still designated by the prefix LM in BS1490, for example LM2 is an alloy of aluminium, silicon and copper. Alloys for casting have a high level of silicon. These will have a tendency to turn black when anodizing, which may cause some difficulties if a constant colour match between extruded and cast sections is required. In the production of the built-in roof rack assembly for the Montego car, for example, the designers experienced difficulty in matching the colour for the cast section clamping the unit down to the body of the car with the rest of the extruded sections forming the roof rack.

Welding of aluminium is now commonly used as a means of jointing sections and can be successfully carried out on site, although the controlled conditions of a factory are often preferable to achieve good quality control. For further information on welding aluminium see Chapter 4. Where finishing is critical, the specification of the filler metal and the process of welding should be adjusted to accommodate the finishing method. Great care should be used in the use of welding in components that are going to be anodized. The filler metal used for welding should match the alloy of the parent metal and if the component is to be anodized it should not contain silicon.

Glazing system for East Croydon Station

The new East Croydon Station, designed by Brookes Stacey Randall and completed in 1992, was designed to serve 14 million passengers a year and is south-east England's busiest through station. The glazing system is an example of a purpose made extrusion used to produce a project-specific assembly, although the overall contract of the new station was under £4 500 000 in 1992.

The structure spans onto the existing abutments at either side of the six railway tracks, creating a 55 m clear space. This minimized disruption to the railway and created a column-free interior. Below the external masted steel structure is a highly glazed envelope, which provides a sophisticated shelter. The glazing system, specially developed by Brookes Stacey Randall for this project, provides maximum transparency yet is robust enough to meet the demands of a railway station.

The glazing system aims to maximize the potential of the toughened glass and the extruded aluminium supporting structure. Each pane of clear toughened glass is only supported at four points. The aluminium extrusion supports the glazing assembly and primarily resists wind loads, which reach 300 mm into the 3 m width of the glass pane thus reducing the effective span to 2400 mm and accessing a beneficial hogging moment. Deflection of the glass is limited to span over 112 by the inboard stainless steel cast arms. The form of the extrusion is elliptical to achieve an elegant and rigid structural form with minimum profile. It is the use of stainless steel castings at the head end of the base, which transforms the essentially linear extrusion into a three-dimensional building component. The East Croydon Glazing System was tested at

Taywood Engineering to BS 5368 as illustrated in Chapter 7.

The extrusion was also designed with front and rear grooves, it is symmetrical and is a well-balanced section. The front groove is used to receive extruded silicone gaskets, acting as closure pieces at wall junctions, and the groove to the rear of the extrusion has been designed to carry door tracks, signage and receive internal glazing, as shown in Figure 2.6. This economical solution is flexible and provides a visual alternative to the standard curtain walling box profile.

The author chose to finish the mast sections with natural anodizing to retain the inherent metal aesthetic of the aluminium together with the benefit of

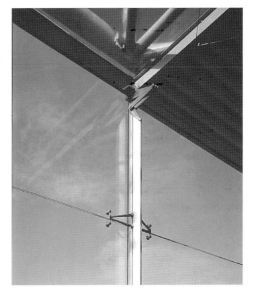

Figure 2.6 East Croydon mullion.

anodizing, which is a very hard fused coating (see pages 27–31). However, care should be taken in it use and the following points noted.

- Ensure significant services are communicated to all concerned – to avoid tongue marks.
- Suitable protection in transit is essential.
- Protection on site from mechanical damage and mortar is also essential. The mortar will cause the anodizing to go permanently 'milky' as a result of an alkaline reaction, which is impossible to reverse.
- Location of the mandrel bridges in extrusions with voids should be agreed, as the chemical structure of the aluminium varies as it re-solidifies after the mandrel. This can form a crystalline or dicroic structure, which has a different reflectance to the section generally, thus modifying the appearance of the anodizing in this zone.
- Die marks – the acceptable level should be agree at the outset and checked on the trial run.

Aspect 2

This patented and fully integrated system of composite cladding panels, windows, doors, louvers and ancillary details, was invented by the author in 1990. Four extruded materials were used in the design and development of the Aspect 2, which is now sold by Corus under the Kal Zip brand.

Figure 2.7 Aspect
Mark 2 integrated
cladding system.

The edges of the panel are formed in PVC-U section to retain the continuous framed EPDM gasket on all sides of the panel. For the purpose of producing a prototype this edge section was produced as an aluminium extrusion due to the speed and relatively low cost of providing an aluminium extrusion for that purpose.

Aspect 2 panels are fixed back via the aluminium clamping plate located within the PVC-U edge section secured by stainless steel machine screws to the aluminium rear extrusions. Thus Aspect 2 is secret fixed and yet every panel is individually removable. A range of aluminium carriers has been developed to accommodate diverse end conditions, i.e. internal and external corners, sill sections, and junctions to dissimilar construction and stop ends.

As each extrusion has been designed a balance has been maintained between the aesthetic requirements of the system, the structural performance of each component, and the limitations of the extruding process. The external corner extrusion is a good illustration of this design process. This component terminates panels from two adjacent elevations and is in effect two stop-ends set at 90° to each other. A client requirement for the extrusion was that it should fit within the maximum CCD of an UK extrusion press.

During 1996 Coseley Panel Products further developed the award winning composite cladding system Aspect 2. Where Aspect 2 used a PVC-U extrusion to form the panel junction and to achieve increased strength and economy, in Aspect 3 this has been replaced by a thermally broken extruded aluminium edge section. This achieves precision and control of tolerance, which is exceptional in panel products. This precision is fundamental to this system of integrated and interchangeable panels, windows and louvers.

Lightweight

Overall weight is a determining factor in car or aircraft design, though some argue this is not critical to architecture. However, weight is a key criterion for a number of reasons as the cost of a section or sheet is primarily determined by the weight of aluminium used. The cost and energy required to transport materials to site is of increasing importance. There are also applications where weight is critical. The choice of aluminium solar shading for the opening section of roof for Chris Lowe's apartment, designed by Brookes Stacey Randall, was governed by the need to minimize the total weight to minimize the power requirement of the hydraulic rams, which operate this roof light. In designing set structures for rock and roll bands, Atelier One maximize the use of aluminium to minimize the weight in transportation. These sets, often costing more than a nursery school or modest train station, are a spectacular form of portable architecture and one fulfilment of an Archigram dream.

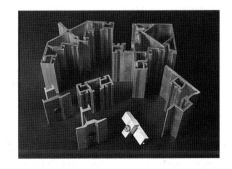

Finishing aluminium

The primary options for finishing aluminium are:

- polyester powder coating
- anodizing

Figure 2.8 The primary aluminium extrusions of the Aspect 2 integrated cladding system.

- PVF2
- mill finish.

The development of finishes for aluminium is an example of sustained R&D within the building industry, and the guarantees offered on 'super durable' polyester powder coating and anodizing represent some of the best product assurance within construction. It is now possible to obtain 25 year guarantees for both finishes, based on testing programmes that include exposure to extreme conditions, including testing for UV stability in the high isolation climates of either Florida or the Middle East. When using polyester powder coating careful specification and monitoring is required to ensure that a thoroughly tested polymer is used and good adhesion achieved.

It is possible to specify polyester powder coating, which includes anti-bacterial agents in the coating. This will kill common bacteria, such as *Escherichia coli*, *Salmonella* and MSRA, which comes into contact with the coated component.

Anodizing is being increasingly specified by architects for its durability and because it allows the metallic quality of the aluminium to remain visible. The durability of anodizing is a direct result of it fusing into the surface of the aluminium forming a hard oxide coating. Early examples of anodized window sections date from the 1930s and are still serviceable. Recent developments have lead to a wide range of colours in anodizing and much tighter

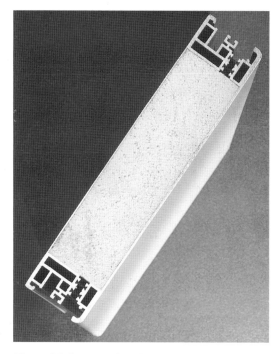

Figure 2.9 Cross-section through an Aspect 3 composite panel.

Figure 2.10 Roof light of Chris Lowe's apartment.

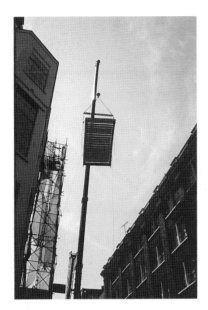

Figure 2.11 Roof light of Chris Lowe's apartment being lifted into position.

Figure 2.12 Ski House by Richard Horden. An example of transportable architecture where lightness was critical and components are used to order and articulate the architecture.

Spar Key Drawing

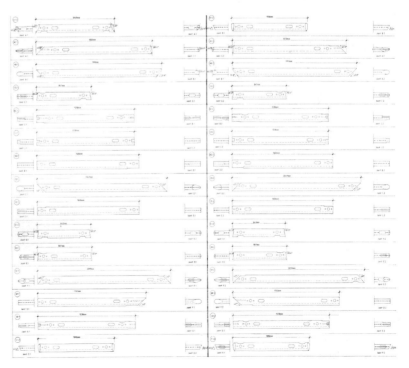

Figure 2.13 Drawing of the extruded aluminium components of the Ski house by architect Richard Horden.

control of colour matching. Anodizing is an electrolytic coating process, and the metal deposit and colour is dependent upon time and current passed. LHT Anodisers use the Unicol system to achieve close control of the colour of the anodizing. The system is based on direct and square wave power source and a process developed in Japan by Nippon Light Metal Co. Few extruders now have in-house anodizing facilities, having mistakenly closed them down with the rise in use of polyester powder coating in the 1980s. However, extrusions that are anodized should be cut to length after that process to remove holding marks unless these can be located discretely within the finished assembly. For this reason it is essential to mark critical visual surfaces on the die drawing.

If a component is left in the anodizing bath too long, not only will the coating be thicker than specified, but more critically the coating becomes soft and durability is reduced. The scratch test developed by Dr Michael Clarke is a relatively straight-forward way for an architect inspecting an anodized assembly for the hardness of the aluminium. Acceptance can be decided from the results of tests made by the method described by Clarke (1985). This test method forms part of BS 6161 part 18, but has not been incorporated into new European Standards.

Natural anodizing can now be closely controlled as a process; therefore the colour should be sufficiently consistent not to require a maximum and minimum colour sample. However, this should be agreed if a specific colour is required, and is essential if a dark colour is to be used. Variation in colour is particularly notice-able in large uninterrupted expanses of flat panels. On the Commerzbank, Foster & Partners used natural anodizing but carefully designed the facades to avoid this potential pit fall. This is achieved by the overall plan of the articulation of the facades and the placement of the anodized components. The control of the alloy quality is critical, as is the orientation of the grain of the sheet aluminium, which is a rolled product. On the Commerzbank, Foster & Partners worked closely with the curtain walling suppliers, Gartners.

Aluminium can be used in the extruded form, know as 'mill finish', the aluminium oxidizes in the atmosphere forming a relatively stable oxide layer. This is not sufficient protection for a corrosive or marine environment and has a relatively consistent grey appearance, which can be described as sugary. Marine cast aluminium component is often specified as polished, which can be an expensive finish and needs regular maintenance.

Maartin van Severens, who trained as an architect prior to concentrating on furni-ture design, seeks perfection in form and detail. The material used appears to be secondary to his formal intent and is expressed primarily in the way it is finished. On the Low Cupboard as shown in Figure 2.15, the combination of aluminium extrusions and sheet aluminium has a simple waxed finish.

Recycling

Compared to the production of aluminium from bauxite by the smelting process, recycling aluminium requires only 5% of the energy. The latest recycling technology can produce aluminium alloy that will match the chemical composition of primary aluminium. There are several UK plants now engaged in recycling aluminium, such as Deeside Aluminium, producing top quality extrusion billet from recycled aluminium. Roof sheets manufactured from 100% recycled alloy were introduced by Hoogovens (now Corus) in 1997. This option is both environmentally sound and economical.

The recycling of aluminium drink cans is now a socially accepted and profitable activity, yet in 1996 only 28% of drink cans were recycled. The constraint is in recovery rather than the process, since the UK built Europe's first dedicated aluminium can recycling plant at Warrington. In the construction industry during 1996, however, approximately 70% of aluminium used was recycled. Yesterday's plank suspended ceiling is, potentially, tomorrow's innovative mullion. Perhaps the can of Coke or beer you drank the other day was used as a curtain walling mullion on a 1960's office building, and, recycled again, could be part of your next project.

Figure 2.14 Commerzbank (architect Foster & Partners).

Figure 2.15 Low cupboard by Maartin van Severens.

Reference

Clarke M., *Trans. Inst. Metal Finish.* 1985; 62: 70–73.

Design guidance

- 2nd edition of Standard & Guide to Good Practice for Curtain Walling issued by Centre for Window and Cladding Technology, 30.9.96.
- CAB guide to Thermal Properties of Aluminium Curtain Walling. The thermal performance of the building envelope remains a mystery to some designers

and the source of building failure. This guide sets out to provide a working method and highlight good design.

- TALAT CD ROM. EC-supported, 13-volume lecture series on aluminium application technology. TALAT is the Training in Aluminium Applications Technology and European Aluminium Association, and the National Aluminium Associations including Aluminium Federation (see below) produced the lecture series.
- Aluminium Federation supplies advice on the use of aluminium, through its Information Service (Tel. 0121 456 1103).
- Properties of Aluminium and its Alloys (2000) Aluminium Federation.
- Finishing Aluminium (a Guide for Architects) by Aluminium Finishers Association, 1999 (Tel. 0121 456 1103).
- BS 1473. 1972 specification for wrought aluminium and aluminium alloys – rivet, bolt and screw stock.
- BS 39871997 Specification for anodic oxidation coatings on wrought aluminium for external architectural applications.
- BS 6161 Part 18 : 1991 (1997) Determination of surface abrasion resistance.
- BS 4300 (parts 10, 11 & 13). 1969 specification (supplementary series) for wrought aluminium and aluminium alloys.
- BS 8118 Structural Use of Aluminium Parts 1 & 2 1991 (replaces CP118 1969, which remains current to allow an overlap in design to take place).

• EN 485 (parts 1–4)	Aluminium and aluminium alloys – Sheet strip and plate
EN 515	Aluminium and aluminium alloys – Wrought products – Temper designations
EN 586 (parts 1 & 2)	Aluminium and aluminium alloys – Forgings
EN 573 (parts 3 & 4)	Aluminium and aluminium alloys – Chemical composition of wrought products
EN 603 (parts 1 & 2)	Aluminium and aluminium alloys – Wrought forging stock
EN 604 (parts 1 & 2)	Aluminium and aluminium alloys – Cast forging stock
EN 754 (parts 1 to 8)	Aluminium and aluminium alloys – Cold drawn rod/bar and tube
EN 755 (parts 1 to 8)	Aluminium and aluminium alloys – Extruded rod/bar and tube
pr EN 755 (parts 9)	Aluminium and aluminium alloys – Extruded rod/bar and tube Part 9 Profile, tolerances on dimensions and form
EN 1301 (parts 1 to 3)	Aluminium and aluminium alloys – Drawn wire
EN 1559 (part 1)	Founding – technical conditions of delivery – Part 1: General

pr EN 1559 (part 4)	Founding – technical conditions of delivery – Part 4: Additional requirements for aluminium castings.
pr EN 1592 (parts 1 to 4)	Aluminium and aluminium alloys – HF seamwelded tubes
EN 1676	Aluminium and aluminium alloys – Alloyed ingots for remelting – Specifications
pr EN 1706	Aluminium and aluminium alloys – Castings – Chemical composition and mechanical properties
pr EN 12020 (parts 1 & 2)	Aluminium and aluminium alloys – Extruded precision profiles in alloys EN AW 6060/EAW 6063
• BS EN 683 (parts 1–3)	1996/7 Aluminium and aluminium alloys – Finstock
• BS EN 1386	1997 Aluminium and aluminium alloys – Treadplate Specifications
• BS EN 1715 (parts 1–5)	1998 Aluminium and aluminium alloys – Drawing Stock

2.2 Flexible Polymer Extrusions

Flexible polymer extrusions are formed from materials that are generally known as rubber, which now range from natural rubber to polymers such as EPDM or silicone. However, some flexible plastics, such as PVC, should also be included. The main reasons for selecting a flexible polymer are:

- to create a seal, supply forces in tension and compression indefinitely;
- to accommodate movement;
- to absorb vibration and noise, acting as an isolator;
- to act as a thermal break as flexible polymers have a low thermal conductivity;
- to provide electrical isolation or conductivity;
- for the feel, flexible polymers typically have frictional properties similar to human skin;
- colour, depending on the polymer required.

Definition of Hardness

A key quality of a flexible polymer is its harness or softness. This can be defined as the 'shore hardness', measured in degrees on the IRHD range, were 20° is very soft, like a foam, and 98° is hard like nylon. The ball of your thumb is typically 25°, a white Staedtler eraser 55° , and a bath plug typically 95° (comparative results are provided by Harbro Rubber Company). In comparison the primary gaskets of Aspect 3 are shore hardness 60°. The American nomenclature

Table 2.4 Material properties of EPDM

Property	Value
Density	1230 kg/m^3
Young's Modulus	5.9×10^{-3} kN/mm^2
Thermal conductivity	0.075–0.18 W/m°C
Coefficient of thermal expansion	150×10^{-6}–450×10^{-6} per °C
Corrosion resistance	Excellent*
Melting point	> 130°C
Recyclability	Moderate/poor
Primary embodied energy[†]	184 GJ/m^3

*Fair/poor in the presence of hydrocarbons.
[†]Data supplied by BRE.

for hardness is Shore A; where 10A is very soft and 90A is hard. It is possible to mould silicone at 10A, but 30A is the practical limit for extruding silicone.

The hardness of a 'rubber' compound is varied primarily by the addition of fillers and reinforcing agents. In the compound of a silicone extrusion the primary filler is fumed silica, which has a very small particle size. BS 5176 and ASTM D2000 provide a framework for the specification elastomers. Both standards use the same eight-character code, which classifies an elastomer including grade, material type, hardness, and special requirements.

Dual hardness extrusions

It is possible and practical to extrude sections which comprise sections of more than one shore hardness; for example, a gasket with a 'hard' foot for security of location and a 'soft' head for compression and seal. Compatible polymers can be combined in a section to take advantage of deferring material properties, including colour. Closed cell foamed sections can be produced on solid elastomer carriers. The horizontal rear air seals of Aspect 3 are an example of a dual hardness EPDM gasket with a 90° shore foot and a closed cell foam EPDM head.

Elastomeric pressure

A well-designed gasket produces an air and water seal by generating elastomeric pressure (see Figure 2.16). This is the result of the compression or displacement of the original form of the gasket. Taking the primary seal of the Don Reynolds' system or Stoakes' Astrawall as an example, it is the displacement of the form of the gasket that produces the seal. It can prove very difficult to produce an airtight seal using a pre-formed gasket on a building scale, by displacement only. The primary weather and air seals in cladding and curtain wall are subjected to cyclic loading of wind pressure and suction. Therefore, the primary gasket should only be considered as 'the first line of defence' against weather penetration. This has led to the development of drainage continuity and pressure equalization in curtain walling and cladding systems. Thus in many curtain walling systems it is the rear air seals which are critical to weatherablity and air infiltration rate. In the design of a rear air seal the gasket is usually compressed by the fixing to produce a seal. Set and creep should be considered in its design and the selection of the hardness of compound to be use. Short time compression set is defined in BS903.

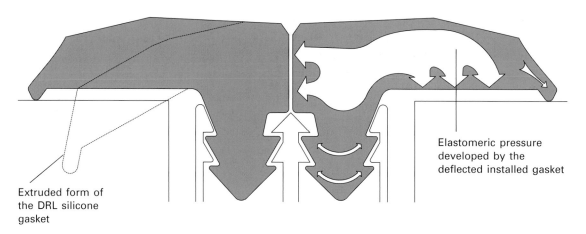

Extruded form of
the DRL silicone
gasket

Elastomeric pressure
developed by the
deflected installed gasket

Figure 2.16 Elastomeric pressure as demonstrated by the primary gasket of the Don Reynolds System.

The design of a gasket is not an exact science and is more a product of experience, trial and error; it is a process of design, testing and development. The gaskets for the Aspect system were designed by Brookes Stacey Randall working with Varnamo Rubber. Figure 2.17 shows the stages of development.

Four dies were needed to produce the final production run of the primary gasket for Aspect 2, which is still in use in Aspect 3. The first gasket had two engineered hinge points that resulted in too little elastomeric pressure being developed. This gasket was also too 'fine' for the range of joint size resulting from component and site assembly tolerances. The second gasket modified the hinge point and was intended to provide a 'set' of the gasket to ensure a successful compressed form. This proved not to be the case. The form of the third die resulted from close examination of the material properties of the EPDM. The next six gasket profiles were a result of modifying the way the same steel die plate is used in the extrusion process, by varying the ram pressure, the vacuum calibration, and the speed at which the gasket is pulled from the extruder. The final production die

DEVELOPMENT OF CAM2 GASKETS
0   55mm

Figure 2.17 Development of the Aspect 2 primary gasket.

was necessary to ensure that the successful gasket profile could be produced
regularly and at economic speeds. The
section of a gasket is usually checked by
a small cross-section, say 2–3 mm deep,
being placed on an epidiascope and
compared to a 10–times full size drawing
of the gasket profile.

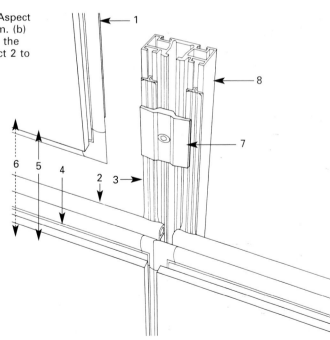

Figure 2.18 The main gaskets of the Aspect 2 system.

Formed and framed gaskets

It is possible to provide drainage continuity using linear flexible extrusions only,
typically by layering the gaskets. Particular care should be taken to ensure that
gaskets are not over-stretched during
installation, otherwise there is a danger that they will shrink back potentially
leaving a gap at a critical point. It is possible to form pre-formed extruded gaskets

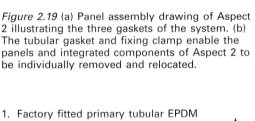

Figure 2.19 (a) Panel assembly drawing of Aspect 2 illustrating the three gaskets of the system. (b) The tubular gasket and fixing clamp enable the panels and integrated components of Aspect 2 to be individually removed and relocated.

1. Factory fitted primary tubular EPDM gasket with moulded tubular corners
2. Dual hardness EPDM horizontal air seal
3. EPDM vertical air seal
4. PVC-U edge section (grey) Welvic R67-915
5. Coated metal panel skin
6. Standard core – extruded polystyrene
7. Extruded aluminium clamping plate Stainless steel Allen head machine screw fixed to an extruded rear block with captive stainless steel Nylock
8. Extruded aluminium rear carrier

Table 2.5 Comparative table of flexible polymers (courtesy of the Harboro Rubber Company)

	NATURAL RUBBER	SBR	EPDM	NEOPRENE CR	HYPALON* CSM
COST FACTOR	1	1	1	2	3
HARDNESS RANGE	30–95°C	40–95°C	30–85°C	30–90°C	40–85°C
COLOURS	Full Range	Full Range	Limited Range	Full Range	Limited Range
HEAT RESISTANCE (°C)					
Maximum Continuous	75°C	100°C	85°C	115°C	130°C
180°C	150°C	180°C			
Maximum Intermittent	110°C	115°C	205°C	300°C	125°C
LOW TEMPERATURE RESISTANCE	–60°C	–55°C	–50°C	–40°C	–25°C
(special grades – 80°C)					
RESISTANCES					
Oxidation	Fair	Fair	Excellent	Very Good	Excellent
Ozone & Weathering	Poor	Poor	Outstanding	Very Good	Outstanding
OIL RESISTANCE					
*ASTM Oil No. 1@ 20°C	Poor	Poor	Fair	Excellent	Excellent
ASTM Oil No. 3 @ 20°C	Unsatisfactory	Unsatisfactory	Unsatisfactory	Good	Excellent
UEL RESISTANCE					
*ASTM FUEL B @ 40°C	Unsatisfactory	Unsatisfactory	Unsatisfactory	Poor	Poor
low temps)					
SOLVENT RESISTANCE					
(20°C) Alcohol	Good	Good	Good	Good	Good
Acetone	Fair	Fair	Good	Fair	Fair
Benzene	Unsatisfactory	Unsatisfactory	Unsatisfactory	Unsatisfactory	Unsatisfactory
CHEMICAL RESISTANCE	Acids	Fair	Fair	Good	Good
Good					
Bases	Good	Good	Good	Fair	Good
PHYSICAL STRENGTH	Excellent	Good	Good	Good	Good
COMPRESSION SET	Good	Good	Good	Fair to Good	Fair
TEAR & ABRASION RESISTANCE	Excellent	Good	Good	Good	Good
RESILIENCE	Excellent	Good	Very Good	Very Good	Fair
PERMEABILITY TO GASES	Poor	Fairly Low	Fairly Low	Low	Low
ELECTRICAL STRENGTH	Excellent	Excellent	Excellent	Good	Good
FLAME RESISTANCE	Poor	Poor	Poor	Self-extinguishing	Good
WATER RESISTANCE	Very Good	Good	Excellent	Good	Very Good

The aromatic content of oils has a moderate swelling effect on rubber. ASTM oil no. 1 (flash point 243°C, aniline point 124°C) has a swelling effect. ASTM oil no. 3 (flash point 163°C, aniline point 124°C) has a severe swelling effect. Both oils are petroleum based and are fully described in ASTM D471.

***Bayer registered trade mark.
**Monsanto registered trade mark.
*Du Pont registered trade mark.

NITRILE NBR	ACRYLIC ACM	VAMAC*	SANTO-PRENE**	SILICONE Si	THERBAN*** HNBR	VITON* F PM	FLUORO-SILICONE FSi
2	4	4	4	6	8	15	40
40–100°C	50–85°C	45-90°C	50–100°C	40–80°C	50–95°C	50–95°C	40–80°C
Limited Range	Black	Limited Range	Full Range	Limited Range	Limited Range	Limited Range	Limited Range
150°C	95°C	125°C	130°C	160°C	100°C	130°C	150°C
160°C	205°C	300°C	180°C	200°C			
–20°C	–20°C	–40°C	–40°C	–60°C	–30°C	–20°C	–60°C
Good	Excellent	Excellent	Good	Excellent	Excellent	Outstanding	Excellent
Fair	Excellent	Excellent	Good	Outstanding	Very Good	Outstanding	Outstanding
	Excellent	Excellent					
100°C Excellent	100°C Excellent						
Excellent	150°C Good	125°C Good	Excellent	Excellent	Excellent	Excellent	Excellent
Excellent	100°C Good	100°C Fair	Fair	Good	Fair	Excellent	Excellent
Fair	Poor	Unsuitable	Poor	Unsuitable	–	Excellent	Fair (good at
Good	Good	Fair	Good	Good	Excellent	Good	Good
Unsatisfactory	Unsatisfactory	Fair	Unsatisfactory	Fair	Good	Unsuitable	Unsatisfactory
Unsatisfactory	Unsatisfactory	Unsatisfactory	Unsatisfactory	Unsatisfactory	Fair	Good	Good
Very Good	Good	Poor	Fair	Good	Fair	Good	Excellent
Fair	Poor	Good	Very Good	Fair	Good	Good	Fair
Good	Good	Good	Good	Poor	Good	Good	Poor
Good	Good	Fair	Fair	Good	Good	Good	Good
Good	Good	Good	Good	Poor	Very Good	Good	Poor
Good	Poor	Fair	Good	Good	Fair	Fair	Fair
Low	Low	Very Low	Fairly Low	Fairly Low	Good	Very Low	Fairly Low
Poor	Fair	Good	Excellent	Excellent	Poor	Good	Excellent
Poor	Poor	Fair	Retardent Grades Available	Good	Poor	Self-extinguishing	Self-extinguishing
Good	Poor	Good	Good	Good	Very Good	Good	Good

39

into a curved profile by forming over a mandrel in steam. A gasket used to seal and retain a car windscreens is a familiar example. A representative minimum radius is 100 mm, but is dependent on the section of the gasket. Too tight a radius and the gasket will wrinkle. Typically the ends of the gasket are butted and vulcanized to form a secure junction that remains flexible. Gaskets can be vulcanized on site, as used on the Sainsbury Centre (see later). To achieve a sharp corner it is necessary to use a moulded corner. The extruded gasket lineals, with clean cut ends, are placed in a steel die and the polymer is injected or shot into the die, forming the corner section and bonding to the extruded gasket. Maintaining continuity of elastomeric pressure at the corner is a key design consideration. The moulded corners of the Don Reynolds' system achieved this by the introduction of a small radius on elevation of the bulb-like 'nose of the gasket'. The moulded corner of the Aspect 2 primary gasket was a particular challenge, as it needed to be tubular to provide mechanical properties similar to the extruded gasket.

Type of elastomers

There are a wide range of potential materials from which to form extruded and moulded flexible components. The following is a brief review of possible elastomers.

Natural rubber

Despite the development of synthetic polymers there is much to commend natural rubber or polyisoprene. This harvestable and renewable elastomer is available in the widest range of hardnesses; it is very strong, naturally self-reinforcing, and is extremely resilient. In a word it is very rubbery. Its limitations are poor resistance to oils and organic fluids, and it has a tendency to perish in open air. This is accelerated if natural rubber is exposed to ozone, and is particularly pronounced if the rubber is also under tension. Car window gaskets dating from before the mid-1970s often demonstrate ozone cracking at the tight radius top corners where the outer flange of the gasket is in tension.

EPDM

Ethylene propylene diene monomer, this polymer offers excellent weather resistance and is now widely used to form gaskets and roof sheeting material. It was originally developed in the 1950s as a compound for the production of tyres. It is resistant to ozone attack and most water-based chemicals, and it remains stable up to 130°C. EPDM offers excellent stability when exposed to UV light, but is susceptible to attack by oil and oil-based products. Predominately specified as black, it has a limited colour range unlike silicones. EPDM can be formed into compounds using fillers, other than carbon black, to provide strong colours, but this may limit UV stability and mechanical properties, and therefore a clear specification and direct dialogue with the producer is essential.

Silicone

Frederick Stanley Kipping (1863–1949) Chair of Chemistry, Nottingham University carried out the ground breaking research into silicon as part of a long chain molecule. When Kipping commenced his research into 'organic compounds', i.e. long chain molecules which contain carbon, most scientists believed that silicon was purely inorganic. Kipping became convinced that silicon could also form long

Figure 2.20 Neil Armstrong stepping onto the moon's surface protected by silicone rubber boots.

Figure 2.21 Black silicone seals, nominally 10 mm wide, between the sheets of toughened glass of the facetted glazing of Western Morning News by Nicholas Grimshaw and Partners.

chain molecular structures, and he devoted 45 years of research to what he described as his 'sticky messes'. Kipping, now regarded as the father of organosilicone chemistry, was pursuing somewhat introspective and purely scientific research, which some would now describe as 'blue sky research'. In 1939 he retired to Caernarvonshire unaware of the impact that his work would have: from the silicone rubber soles of Neil Armstrong's boots, as he stepped onto the moon in 1969, to the wet applied seal of the gap between two sheets of toughened glass.

Glass is silicon based (made primarily form silica, or sand), it is temperature and moisture resistant, chemically inert, and dielectric. Plastics are primarily carbon based; they are strong and can be produced in many forms. Silicones combine the advantages of both glass and plastics, and are unique materials not found in nature. In 1931 the development of silicone was taken up in the USA by Coring Glass and was transferred to the Mellon Institute of Industrial Research in 1937. Here a team of scientists, including McGregor and Hyde, working under fellowships from the Corning Glass Works, developed usable silicone polymers. In 1940 Corning involved Dow Chemical and in 1942 the first Dow Corning silicone product was sold for sealing aircraft engine ignitions. In 1943 the Dow Corning Corporation was formed.

The Second World War may have accelerated the development of silicone compounds but its origins lie in the realms of pure science and a material supplier to the construction industry. Although silicone rubbers were developed by Dr Earl Warrick and first successfully produced at the end of 1943, it was not until 1958 that gun applied silicone sealants were introduced to the construction industry, following research by Remo Maneri for Dow Corning (Anon, 1993). Silicone can be wet applied, extruded and moulded, and offers excellent durability in an operating range typically from –60°C to +205°C. It can be produced almost transparent and coloured to any RAL number if the quantity required is sufficient.

Neoprene

The short lifespan of natural rubbers, especially when exposed to ozone and UV light acted as the stimulus for the development of polychloroprene by the Du Pont Company in the 1930s under the trade name 'Neoprene'. For many architects and engineers 'Neoprene' has become the generic term for all types of polychloroprene. Jean Prouvé in detailing the Maison du Peuple Clichy (1937–39) and his designs for curtain walling assemblies (1938–39) anticipated the use of neoprene gaskets in curtain walling although it was not yet commercially available. The first patent for window construction using neoprene seals was filed in the United States on 22nd April 1938 (US patent number 2205538) and was simply entitled 'window construction'. The inventor was William Owen on behalf of Pittsburgh Plate Glass Co. Pennsylvania. General Motors realized that elastomeric seals represented a more practical method of weather proofing car windscreens, and pioneered the development of 'zipper gaskets'.

The first well-documented installation of this type on a building, was on the Harrisburg West Interchange Turnpike Booths in Pennsylvania, in 1949. Alan

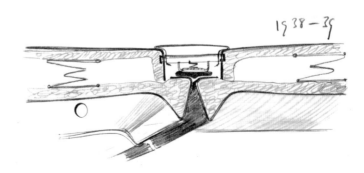

Figure 2.22 Horizontal panel junction of La Maison du Peuple Clichy by Jean Prouvé.

Brookes (1985) noted that 'The gaskets on this project are still providing sound weathering and structural retention'. Possibly the first major building to use neoprene gaskets was the General Motors Technical Centre Detroit, by Eero Saarenien, in 1953. The first block constructed in 1951 soon leaked, as the sealant caulking failed to adhere to either the aluminium framing or the panelling, which was glass and vitreous enamel. General Motors, based on its experience with gaskets in the automobile industry, applied its resources to solving the problem and produced a weather seal similar to that use on the Harrisburg Turnpike booths. This zipper-type gasket allowed the glass to be accurately positioned within the aluminium framing before pressure was applied via the gasket. The gaskets appear to have been butted and glued; vulcanized corners were a later development. These gaskets were not continuously stretched around a curved corner as in a car windscreen. In total, 4600 m of neoprene gaskets were installed at the General Motors Technical Centre.

General Motors patented the 'H' section gasket with sealing strips for building applications in 1955, and Russell Bush was named as the inventor. In the UK the first 'H' section gaskets were used on the Commercial Union Assurance building in Manchester by Gollins, Melvin, Ward and Partners, and shortly after by architects Farmer and Park on the Fawley Power Station. During the 1960s Miles Redfern (now Leyland and Birmingham Rubber Co) and Richard Stoakes of Astrawall (now Stoakes Systems) developed structural neoprene gaskets. The

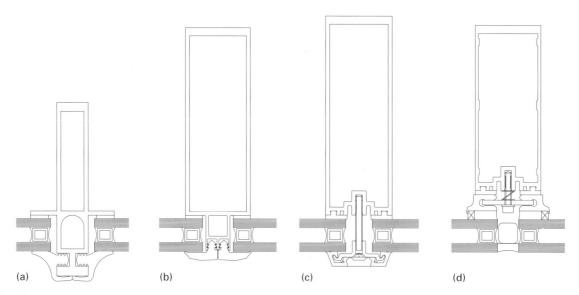

Figure 2.23 (a) Presslock, (b) Don Reynolds, (c) Stoakes Systems gasket cladding and curtain walling systems with (d) Stoakes Systems silicone bonded curtain walling.

CLASP and MACE building consortium programmes enabled Miles Redfern to develop the practical application of neoprene gaskets.

In the early 1970s, Modern Art Glass Ltd, in consortium with Leyland and Birmingham Rubber Co and Aluminium Systems of Dublin, developed the 'Pressure Glaze' and the 'Presslock' systems using structural neoprene sections. These were specified by Farrell and Grimshaw for Herman Miller Factory Bath and Winwick Quay, Warrington. This consortium was responsible for the development of the neoprene gaskets at the Sainsbury Centre for the Visual Arts at UEA by Foster Associates, completed in 1976. This lattice of gaskets seals an interchangeable system of panels, louvers, and glazing that form the roof and side walls. The continuous network of gaskets was vulcanized on site joining 14 panel modules together, thus sealing the entire 131 × 35 m building with a single ladder gasket. This component of a lightweight architecture weighed over 20 tonnes.

The patent for 'lattice gaskets' was granted to Ron Howorth on 26th November 1980 (UK patent no. 1580053). If it is necessary to join gaskets on site, vulcanization or the formation of chemical cross-linking generally remains preferable to bonding due to difficulties of adhesion, peel, and the maintenance of consistent flexibility or shore hardness.

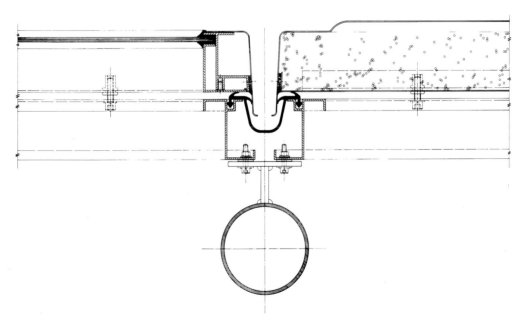

Figure 2.24 Sainsbury Centre by Foster Associates (now Foster & Partners): original panel detail.

In 1983 Don Reynolds was granted a patent for a curtain walling system using a face applied gasket. By the late 1980s, a DTI report noted that Don Reynolds Ltd had become one of the leading exporters of curtain walling from the UK, based essentially on a single design idea, i.e. a structural silicone gasket, in a market otherwise dominated by European curtain walling companies. The structural silicone gaskets for this system were developed by Don Reynolds, primarily with Dow Corning and extruded by Silicone Altimex. By using silicone extrusions, Don Reynolds Ltd was able to offer a range of gaskets with guaranteed weatherablity and physical stability between −60°C and +200°C, in a range of colours.

Figure 2.25 Installation of the ladder gasket at the Sainsbury Centre.

Roof membranes

PVC and EPDM have in the past 30 years become a reliable means of producing durable flat roofs. PVC roof membranes benefit from good stability and their ability to accommodate movement. Sarnafil PVC roofing, for example, can be stretched by 200%. They are produced by coating onto a glass or polyester carrier, which is rolled for delivery to site. The use of polyvinyl chloride has been criticized, however, due to the environmental concerns associated with chlorine. This has led to an increased use of EPDM and the development of polyolefines.

Polyethylene and polypropylene are familiar examples of polyolefines, as they are thermosetting plastics they can readily be recycled. Polyolefine roofing membranes are produced by dual extrusion onto a carrier or reinforcement. The Sarna process for producing a stress free sheet has been patented. The carrier is either a glass fibre scrim or a combination of glass fibre and synthetic scrim depending on the proposed application of the roof membrane. The long service life of the polyolefines, such as Sarnifil T material when used as roof sheeting, means that recyclablity is possibly not a primary consideration. Sarna, the manufacturers of Sarnifil T material, recycle scrap within the manufacturing process and will recycle site scrap on request.

The interface of PVC and EPDM should be carefully detailed and handled, as solvents used in the preparation of EPDM can degrade the PVC.

The Festo 'Airtecture'

The Swabian company Festo has used a range of elastomeric sheet materials to create a transportable exhibition pavilion. Festo describes it as 'Airtecture', as this pneumatic building achieves its structural rigidity from tubular elements containing compressed air. The pressure is computer controlled and responds to changes in wind loading monitored by weather sensors.

The wall structure comprises 40 Y-shaped compressed air columns. Each is tied down with an elastic tension element formed from polyamide fabric with an internal silicone hose. This muscle-like component responds to wind force on the side walls and contracts. The wall structure and opaque wall sections are formed from of a double layer of hypalon (chlorosulphonated polyethylene) coated polyamide. Between each bay is a transparent slot formed from two layers of hostaflon ET (trade name Velaglas). The roof stability is achieved by alternating elements of positive (500 mbar) and negative (2.5 mbar) pressure. This is considered to be the first use of pressurized and partially evacuated chambers to produce a roof structure. The translucent and evacuated sections in the roof are formed from two layers of an innovative translucent elastomer of ethylene acetate (trade name Levapren) on polyester, which is specified under the product name Vitroflex.

The pavilion was designed by Festo's Head of Corporate Design, Axel Thallemer Dipl.-Ing., and manufactured by DSB-Eschershausen. It is intended to reflect Festo's core business, i.e. air.

Figure 2.26 Festo 'Airtecture' Exhibition Pavilion.

Figure 2.27 Detail of the Festo 'Airtecture' Exhibition Pavilion showing the Y-shaped compressed air columns and 'muscle'-like tension element.

Figure 2.28 Interior of the Festo 'Airtecture' Exhibition Pavilion.

The pavilion, first erected in Esslingen, can be packed into a standard 12-m container and readily transported, as it weighs in total only 6 tonnes.

References and further information

Anon (1993). 'The human spirit is a pioneering spirit', 50 years of Dow Corning, Dow Corning Corporation.

Brookes, A. (1985). Development and use of gaskets in cladding system. In *Roofing Cladding and Insulation.*

CIRIA (1998). Sealant joints in the external envelope of buildings. *A Guide to Design, Specification and Construction.*

Jenkins, M. (1984). A study of patent with particular reference to gasket joints in curtain walling. Liverpool University Dissertation.

Lambot, I. (ed.) (1989). *Buildings and Projects 1971–1978.* Norman Foster, Foster Associates. Watermark.

Prouvé, J. ('constructeur') (1901–1984). Exhibition Catalogue Centre, George Pompidou, October 1990 ISBN 2-85850-554-3.

BS 903	Physical testing of rubber
BS 1154 (1997)	Specification for natural rubber compounds
BS 2751 (1990)	Specification for general purpose acryonitrile-butadiene rubber compounds
BS 2752 (1997)	Specification for chloroprene rubber compounds
BS 5176 (1996)	Specification for classification systems for vulcanized rubbers

2.3 Rigid Polymer Extrusions

Rigid polymer extrusions are produced by two primary techniques: extrusion or pultrusion. The method used depends on the material and is flexibility when semi-molten. PVC-U is extruded, whereas glass fibre reinforced plastic or carbon fibre composites are pultruded.

PVC-U extrusions

Replacement windows with PVC-U frames have become a ubiquitous component of domestic construction in Europe. It is predominantly used in white, although it is extruded in black, grey and even a brown wood effect, produced via a foil process. But how well understood is PVC-U as a material? It is valued for its durability and low maintenance, and it is relatively straightforward to form a weatherproof window in PVC-U, as it can readily be welded to itself. However, it is relatively flexible with a Young's Modulus of approximately 2500 N/mm^2. This does not present a problem in modestly sized domestic window although it does lead to a visible face dimension some four times larger that a steel window. To form PVC-U windows of larger dimensions an internal steel rectangular hollow section it used to reinforce the PVC-U window frame. Alternatively the PVC-U section can be co-extruded with a glass fibre reinforced pultruded section.

A die for a PVC-U window section typically cost £35 000–60 000 compared to £1500–2000 for a similar aluminium window section. This is a direct result of the plasticity of PVC-U as it is extruded; it is soft, almost like toothpaste, and as the section leaves the die it is cooled in calibrated chambers which maintain the

Table 2.6 Material properties of PVC-U

Density	1440 kg/m^3
Young's modulus	> 2.5 kN/mm^2
Thermal conductivity	0.18 W/m$^\circ$C
Co-efficient of thermal expansion	50×10^{-6} – 100×10^{-6} per K
Corrosion resistance	Excellent
Melting point	75°C
Recyclability	Good
Primary embodied energy[*]	173 GJ/m^3

[*]Data supplied by BRE.

cross-section and overall straightness of the lineal (see Figure 2.29). The calibration chambers of the die tooling also control tolerances and gloss level of the section. The typical lead-time for a PVC-U die is 10–12 weeks for die trial material with a further 3–5 weeks for production, if no modifications are required. The design of PVC-U sections and the dies for their production, remain largely dependent of the direct experience of key individuals, which at times is jealously guarded for commercial reasons. PVC-U is predominately used as a self-finished material, even when exposed, as it offers good durability and a high degree of UV stability. As PVC-U is a thermoplastic it can be readily recycled, even used sections, as window frames for many years can be recycled if cleaned.

Figure 2.29 Calibrated chambers of a PVC-U die.

PVC-U extrusions are extensively used to form the internal edge details of a composite metal panel system (see Chapter 5 for further discussion of composite panels). PVC-U is selected for its ability to form relatively complex sections, in what is an essentially linear application. PVC-U offers the benefit that it forms an inherent thermal break, with a typical thermal conductivity of approximately 0.2 W/m°C. In comparison to aluminium, PVC-U sections are less precise and a greater tolerance range needs to be taken into account in the design of the component. The Aspect 2 cladding system used a PVC-U section to form the edge of the panel receiving the EPDM gaskets and clamping plate. To achieve a greater consistency and precision Coseley Panel Products now use a thermally broken aluminium section, a rare example of development by direct material substitution. A further advantage of the use of aluminium extrusion in panel production is that can be readily and accurately curved, which is not possible with PVC-U.

PVC-U can be readily injection-moulded, which facilitates the production of weldable complex forms for use with extruded PVC-U. This was used to unite the 'male' and 'female' edge components of Aspect 1 composite cladding panels, arguably a highly sophisticated yet unnecessarily complex piece of design, which the development of Aspect 2 overcame.

The Proteus composite panel systems produced by **ame** uses PVC-U components, produced by Axis Profiles of Liverpool, to form edge sections and interlocking panel junctions. The PVC-U edge section demonstrates how two

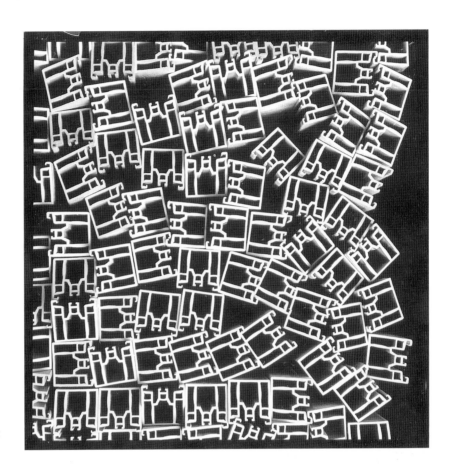

Figure 2.30 The PVC-U edge sections of Aspect 2: Welvic Rg7-915.

extrusions can be used to provided flexibility (see Figure 2.31). The standard edge section has a groove at the rear, which is there solely to receive and lock in a second PVC-U extrusion. This enables **ame** to make panels offering a range of thermal performance or a range of core types at a significantly lower cost, as die costs are directly related to size and complexity. **Ame** also use a PVC-U insert with extruded aluminium window section to enable them to be fully integrated into the Proteus range. The two leading composite manufacturers (thus forming a paradigm of materials selection) Coseley and **ame**, have adopted diametrically opposite views on the use of PVC-U whilst seeking to achieve a similar aesthetic and near identical technical performance.

Figure 2.32 shows an interlocking panel section of Proteus 20. This is a dual hardness extrusion and is a co-extrusion of rigid PVC-U and flexible Nitral. This section has been developed by **ame** to ensure the front primarily horizontal gasket and rear horizontal air seal are kept in place by being fused to the rigid

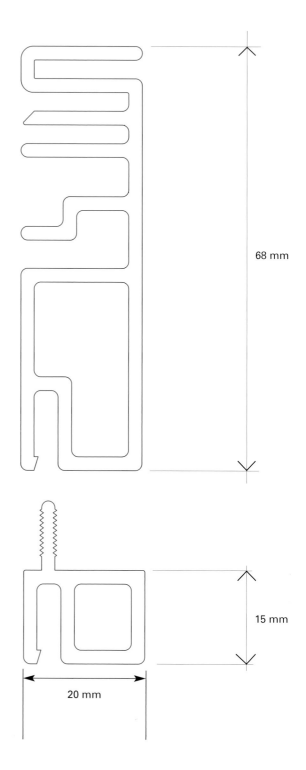

Figure 2.31 Two PVC-U interlocking extrusions used to provided flexibility panel dimensions in **ame**'s cladding systems.

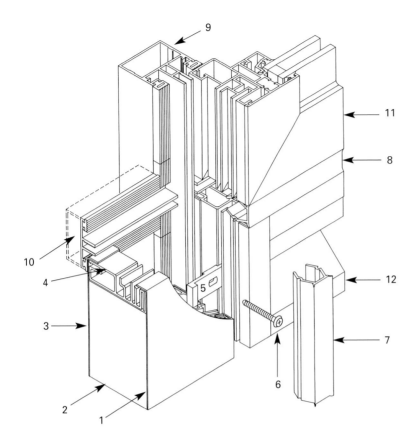

1. Metal outer skin
2. Insulation core –
   foam 70 mm panel
   Rockwool lamella 85 mm
   panel
3. Metal rear skin
4. PVC-U rear skin
5. Fixing cleat
6. Fixing
7. Dual hardness PVC-U/nitral
   vertical gasket
8. Dual hardness PVC-U/nitral
   horizontal gasket
9. Vertical aluminium
   mullion + EPDM gaskets
10. Horizontal alluminium
    transom + EPDM gaskets
11. Integrated window
12. Integrated louvre

Figure 2.32 Proteus 20 integrated cladding system by **ame**.

PVC-U cruciform. The flexibility of the Nitral is essential to form a successful weather seal.

Pultrusions

It is possible to strengthen and modify the stiffness characteristics of a polymer section by reinforcing it with strands of fibres, such as glass or carbon. Why are these sections pultruded rather than extruded? The primary reason for pultruding is to ensure that the fibre orientation is maintained. If one attempted to extrude GRP the glass fibres would buckle and their orientation would effectively

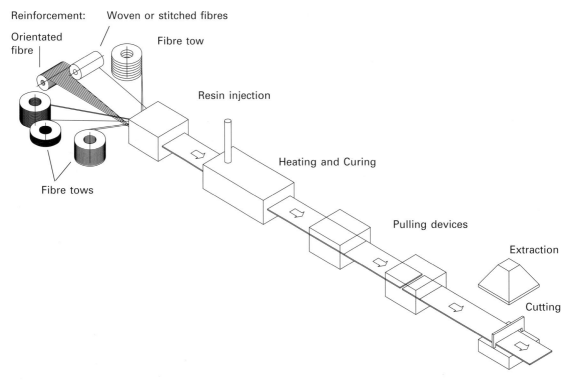

Figure 2.33 The overall pultrusion process.

be random. In comparison with PVC dies, the assembly required for a pultrusion is significantly more expensive. Although the die plate is essentially similar, as the polymer or resin is still extruded, the mandrel needs to incorporate the fibre delivery and drawing mechanism. A typical application of carbon fibre pultrusions includes the plate bonding system for the repairs of failing concrete structures, where the flat carbon fibre sections are delivered to site in large continuous roles. Applications for GRP pultrusions include non-conductive grids or decking for industrial applications and structural sections.

The primary advantages of the use of carbon fibre reinforced resins are:

- high strength to weight ratio
- effectively zero coefficient of thermal expansion
- ability to tailor material properties to the application
- non-corrosive with excellent UV stability.

Currently carbon fibre has the disadvantage of relatively high material cost. Unlike thermoplastic plastics, which can be remoulded, the resins used for carbon fibre-based components are thermosetting. Thermosetting plastics can be disposed of, or reused, in two ways:

• burnt as a solid fuel, usually with domestic refuse
• broken down into simpler products, providing gas and liquid fuels and other useful chemicals.

Flat pultruded carbon fibre sections have achieved a growing acceptance as a method of reinforcing existing concrete structures, replacing steel plating systems. The advantage of the carbon fibre is that it has a smaller section size, particularly minimizing the increased depth of the existing structure. The carbon fibre can also be delivered in roll form, avoiding or minimizing jointing when reinforcing a long-span concrete structure. The Sika system uses an epoxy adhesive to bond the carbon fibre to the concrete. The material cost of the carbon fibre is outweighed by the value of the structural repair, and the time and embodied energy saved compared to its replacement. Successful new building applications of pultrusions include applications in oil exploration platforms, non-conductive gratings, and bridge construction.

Figure 2.34 Carbon fibre reinforcement pultrusion manfactured by Sika being bonded to the soffit of Dudley Port Bridge, a reinforced concrete bridge, using an epoxy adhesive, Sikadur 30.

To achieve greater torsional resistance in a pultruded carbon fibre tubular section, the carbon fibres are woven into an interlocking spiral as they are pultruded: a combination of the technology of the textile industry and the extrusion process. It is also possible to introduce woven or stitched fabric reinforcement to provided highly specific strength characteristics with a pultruded section.

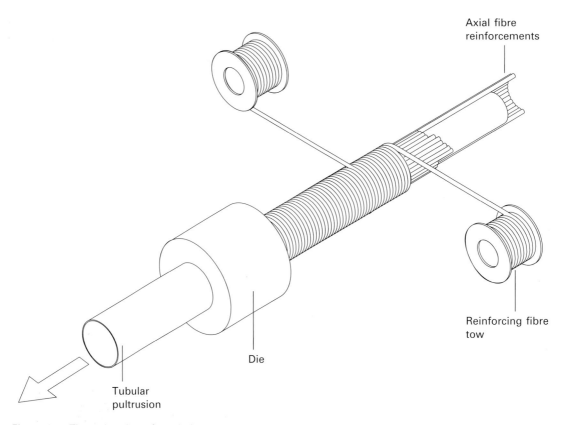

Figure 2.35 The pultrusion of a tubular section: detail nominally at die.

Standards for pultrusions

To encourage the use of pultruded sections and to facilitate specification, a CEN standard has been developed, pr EN 13706, which comprises three parts: Designation methods of test, General requirements, and Specific requirements. The standard seeks to make a pultrusion as readily specifiable as hot rolled steel or extruded aluminium. This is primarily achieved in two ways.

First, by a system of designation, which comprises a description and five data blocks. Block 1 states profile shape, reinforcement materials and additional processes; block 2 states polymer type and specific properties (e.g. fire retardant); block 3 states section modulus, E, in Gpa units. Blocks 4 and 5 are currently empty and are available for future use. Therefore Pultrusion, EN 13706-BGV, IF, E23 is a box section with glass fibre reinforcement, surface veil: isophthalic polyester resin, fire retardant and a section modulus of 23 Gpa.

Second, by recognizing two standard grades for glass reinforced pultrusions, E17 and E23. The next edition of this standard is likely to include a wider range of standard grades.

Fabric restrained pultruded arched truss

Neil Burford and Frazer Smith of the University of Dundee were given the brief to design an improved version of a rapidly deployed lightweight shelter for military vehicles. The existing model weighed 240 kg and took 4 hours to erect. They designed a shelter based around a fabric-restrained elastically-bent pultrusion, which forms an elliptical arch. It can be deployed in 4 minutes and weighs only 90 kg. The flexible linear compression member is a pultrusion only 92 × 13.5 mm with three integral luffing groves. The pultrusion is formed from polyester resin with high modulus E-glass fibres (continuous). Woven scrim close to the surface of the pultrusion is also used to increase shear stiffness and to provide crack resistance. The pultrusion is used in three sections with cast aluminium hinges, primarily to facilitate transportation in a tube, which is stowed in a bag containing the complete shelter, which can readily be carried by four men.

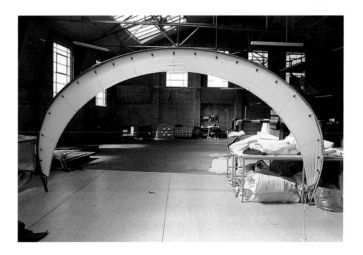

Figure 2.36 Prototype of fabric restrained arched truss designed by Neil Burford and Frazer Smith.

The innovative aspect of this structure is the use of an elliptical fabric web to stiffen the arch. The cutting pattern of the fabric provides the necessary stiffness, and the fabric is set at ±45° to the pultruded compression member thereby defining the geometry of the arch on a totally repeatable basis. This project not only

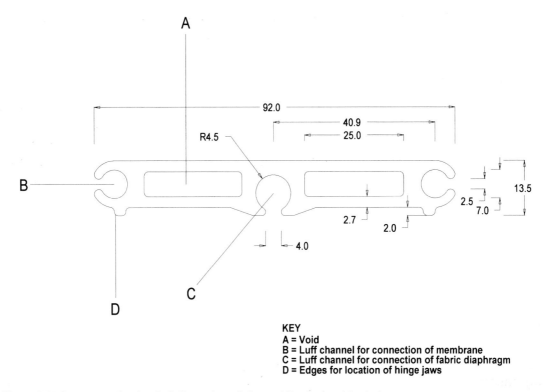

KEY
A = Void
B = Luff channel for connection of membrane
C = Luff channel for connection of fabric diaphragm
D = Edges for location of hinge jaws

Figure 2.37 Geometry of pultruded rib section of the rapidly deployable shelter.

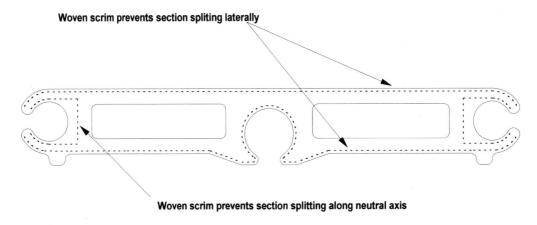

Woven scrim prevents section spliting laterally

Woven scrim prevents section splitting along neutral axis

Figure 2.38 Distribution of woven fibre reinforcement in pultruded section of the rapidly deployable shelter.

demonstrates the potential of lightweight architecture but the inventiveness and benefit of architects and engineers working in close collaboration.

Tapered sections

The pultrusion process, however, can only create linear sections. If a tapered section is required it needs to be formed of pre-impregnated carbon fibre sheet, as would a moulded or formed component. Tapered carbon fibre fishing rods are made by wrapping a pre-impregnated sheet at an angle around a steel mandrel, forming a pattern of spiral reinforcement. Typically, this is then shrink wrapped and set in an autoclave at 180°C. Once the tapered rod cools, the steel mandrel shrinks and drops out.

Design guidance

Rubber and Plastic Research Association (RAPRA) 01939 250383
RAPRA web site is: www.rapra.net
RAPRA provides information including software:
Sensan – entitled 'A Virtual Plastics Consultant'
Flow 2000 – an extrusion simulation software.
Sigmasoft – simulation software for injection moulded components including the cooling and phases of thermoplastics and elastomers.
Composites and Plastics In Construction BRE RAPRA Conference Papers 16–18 November 1999. BRE RAPRA
LC Hollaway & MB Leeming (1999) Strengthening of reinforced concrete structures using externally bonded FRP composites in structural and civil engineering. Woodhead Publishing

pr EN 13706	Reinforced Plastic Composites – Specification for Pultruded Profiles
BS EN 513	Unplasticized polyvinyl chloride (PVC-U) profiles for the fabrication of windows and doors
BS EN 514	Unplasticized polyvinyl chloride (PVC-U) profiles for the fabrication of windows and doors Determination of the strength of welded doors and T-joints
BS ISO 1163	Plastics: Unplasticized polyvinyl chloride (PVC-U) moulding and extrusion material
BS 7412	Specification plastic windows made from PVC-U
BS 7413	Specification for white PVC-U extruded hollow profiles with heat welded corner joints for plastic windows; material Type A
BS 7414	Specification for white PVC-U extruded hollow profiles with heat welded corner joints for plastic windows; material Type B.

2.4 Extruded Steel and other metals

It is possible to extrude metals other than aluminium, including iron, steel, and stainless steel, nickel alloys, and bronze. It is the resistance to deformation of the metal and the available pressure of the ram, which are the controlling factors.

Steel

The extrusion process for steel is identical to aluminium except that the melting point is higher, i.e. 900–1300°C whereas aluminium requires only 500–600°C, and the ram pressure required is greater, section for section. Also, powdered glass is used as a lubricant and insulator to the hot steel billet.

Osborn Steel, for example, has been extruding steel since 1953 and it is now capable of manufacturing thinner and more complex shapes due to advances in the extrusion process and its control. Osborn Steel's press applies a ram pressure of 1200 tonnes. The extrusion process is an alternative to hot rolling, casting, machining or fabricating steel sections. In short to medium runs it is usually more economical than other metal forming processes for linear components. At present there are only a limited number of steel extruders, and maximum CCD in the UK is 140 mm. Once extruded a steel section is allowed to cool before heat treatment, if metallurgically necessary, straightening, and checks for dimensional accuracy.

Table 2.7 Material properties of mild steel (medium carbon)

Property	Value
Density	8002 kg/m^3
Young's modulus	205–210 kN/mm^2
Thermal conductivity	24.3–65.2 W/m°C
Co-efficient of thermal expansion	1.2×10^{-5} per °C
Corrosion resistance	Excellent
Melting point	>> 1300°C
Recyclability	Excellent
Primary embodied energy[*]	274 GJ/m^3

[*]Data supplied by BRE.

(a)

(b)

(c)

(d)

(e)

(f)

(g)

(h)

Figure 2.39 Process of extruding steel at Osborn Steel. (a) Steel billets being cut to size; (b) machining leading edge of billet; (c) boring a billet for a hollow section; (d) billet is heated in an induction furnace; (e) heated billet is rolled in powered glass; (f) billet is inserted in extrusion press; (g) extruded steel section leaving the press; (h) straightening a steel extrusion.

Dies for extruding steel are made from hardened steel. The relative economy and speed of the die production process and the relative ease of modification means that the steel extrusion process is used to produce prototype sections, as in its aluminium counterpart.

It is possible to save time, cost and materials by using an extrusion as compared to machining or fabricating a stainless steel. For medium to short runs extruding a steel component can be more cost effective than casting, particularly noting that in some metals it is difficult to cast long thin sections. Typical applications of steel extrusions include coke oven door seals, finned boiler tubes or lobal pump components. A highly visible application of extruded stainless steel was the replacement of wrought iron glazing bars on Burton and Turner's Palm House at Kew, London. In restoring the Palm House in 1988, the engineers Posford Duvivier sought an economical and durable method of replicating the profile of the original wrought iron bars. Eight-metre lengths of extruded stainless steel were used, a precise sectional replacement for the original bars. They were painted white on site to maintain the original appearance of the Palm House.

Although the process of extruding steel has been refined in the past 40 years, the sections are typically thicker than in aluminium and less intricate. Section for section, in say a glazing bar, steel extrusions can be smaller due to the greater stiffness of steel when compared to a general grade of aluminium. It is possible to extrude a wide range of steel alloys, and grades, including stainless steel. Therefore giving precise design parameters is not possible and should be discussed with the extruder.

Figure 2.40 Section of the glazing bar at the Palm House at Kew.

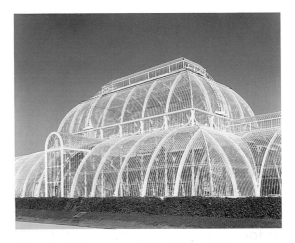

Figure 2.41 The restored Palm House at Kew.

Figure 2.42 Steel
extrusion: typical
design guidance.

Radii:
R = 1.5 mm to 4.5 mm in carbon steel
R = 3 mm to 6 mm in stainless steel
r = 0.75 mm to 1.2 mm in carbon steel
r = 1.5 mm to 2.0 mm in stainless steel

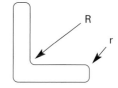

Angularity
Angular tolerance ± 2°

Cross arch or transverse flatness

Transverse flatness
A = 1% of width W or
0.2 s when W is less than 25 mm

Twist
1:500

Camber or bow
1:500

Note: All size limits and tolerances
quoted should be taken as a guide only,
and tolerances appropriate to a particular
section may vary, courtesy Osborn Steel
Extrusions Ltd.

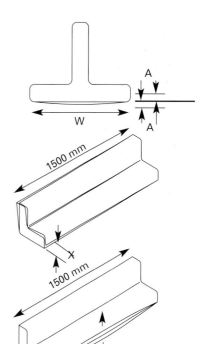

Guidance for an open section includes:

- keep internal and external radii as gradual as possible
- avoid re-entrant angles, as far as possible
- for channel section seek to achieve a 1:1 ratio between breadth and depth.

Typical minimum web thickness is 4 mm, and the recommended minimum corner
is 1.5 mm.

Tolerances are exact; for example, on a solid section with dimensions between 4.5 and 25 mm a tolerance of +0.75 −0 mm is achievable.

Magnesium

This is the lightest metal that can readily be used in construction. Typically it is alloyed with aluminium and zinc. Section 2.1 on aluminium extrusion includes the use of magnesium in aluminium alloys to improve the mechanical properties of an aluminium alloy. Like aluminium, magnesium is only viable because of the formation of a protective oxide layer. Litech Kft of Hungary produce a mountain bike frame comprising welded extruded magnesium tubes; the alloy is 94% magnesium. This frame offers excellent strength to weight ratio, significantly lighter that titanium frames and lighter or equal to a carbon fibre frame.

Noting that magnesium can be readily extracted from seawater, where it is present as magnesium chloride, magnesium is possibly the viable lightweight construction metal of the twenty-first century.

3

Metal Castings

Introduction

Foundries are a fascinating cross between Danté's Inferno and a wonderland of lost components. They offer considerable technical opportunity to an inquisitive architect or engineer. Casting is an affordable route for the reintroduction of craft into the building industry, in the form of a reliable and repeatable manufacturing process, which is based on the skill of the die or pattern maker, the inventiveness of the architect/engineer, and the expertise of the foundry. Castings are a good example of the application of batch production, to match the particular requirements of a building project.

The typical tensile strength of cast iron used in the first half of the nineteenth century was less than 100 N/mm^2. Figure 3.2 (supplied by Dr Nieswaag of TU Delft) shows how this had increased to over 1400 N/mm^2 the 1980s, via key advances in metallurgy. The casting process, linked to rigorous quality control

Table 3.1 Material properties of stainless steel

Property	Value
Density	8000 kg/m^3
Young's modulus	195 t /190 l kN/mm^2
Thermal conductivity	15 W/m°C
Co-efficient of thermal expansion	1.6 × 10^{-5} per °C
Corrosion resistance	Excellent
Melting point	1425°C
Recyclability	Excellent
Primary embodied energy[*]	150 GJ/m^3

[*]Data supplied by BRE.

65

Figure 3.1 The large scale melt at Sheffield Forgemasters.

procedures, can provide reliable components of good integrity, which can be used in highly stressed applications with a better fatigue life than a welded fabrication.

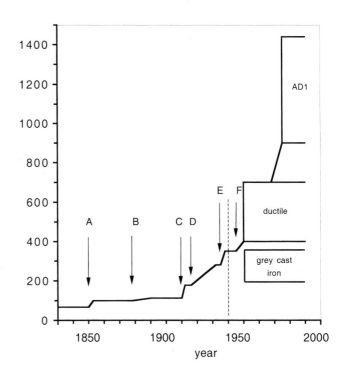

Figure 3.2 The development of the tensile strength of cast iron from the mid-nineteenth century

The past 20 years has seen further advances in casting techniques; the basic challenge for a foundry is to produce castings of a known quality and integrity. The advances in process achieved by each foundry are jealously guarded secrets and are unlikely to be incorporated into British Standards. Architects can benefit from technological advances primarily achieved for defence and aerospace industries or civil engineering applications, such as oil exploration in the North Sea. Cast components can range in size from a 50–tonne steel node of a production platform (a sand casting) to intricate sub-assemblies in missile guidance systems (a lost wax casting). Objects as familiar as the supermarket trolley and public telephones use cast components.

Figure 3.3 A lost wax casting from MBC weighing a few grams.

However, the development of the use of castings within the building industry in recent years, is as significant as the transfer of technology from the defence or aerospace industries. It is unlikely that castings will regain the dominant structural role that they enjoyed in the industrial buildings of the nineteenth century. Castings are increasingly being specified as part of an overall assembly, such as cast nodes of the Renault Centre, the gerberettes of the Centre Pompidou, or the glazing brackets of East Croydon Station.

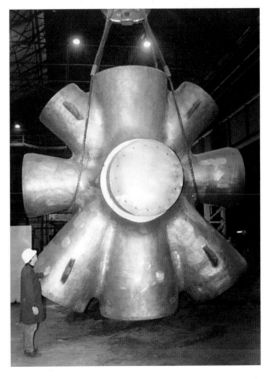

Figure 3.4 A sand casting, a trunnion node for a North Sea oil production platform weighing 75 tonnes.

Why Cast?

The advantages of a casting can be summarized as follows.

- Form: structural and geometrical requirements can be accommodated in a single component.
- Economical use of material: puts the metal where it is required, enabling the sections to be tailored to meet the specific design loads.

Figure 3.5 Gerberettes of the Centre Pompidou, at Krups (architect Piano and Rogers, engineers Ove Arup and Partners).

- Ease of production: once the form and die are established and with appropriate quality assurance, reliable and repeatable components can be readily manufactured.
- Durability: low maintenance components.
- High quality of finish: this is dependent on the type of casting method, for example lost wax castings provide very fine finishes.
- Fine tolerances: this is dependent on the casting method.

Castings are an affordable option, offering the architect or engineer considerable freedom to form the 3D component, which can produce elegant and expressive elements. Lost wax castings were used in the suspending elements of Parc de la Villette 'Les Serres' or Bioclamatic facades because 'the freedom of form allowed by the casting process permits the piece to resolve a number of complicated assemblies and geometry problems with one form in the shape of a bird' (Dutton and Wernick, 1992; p. 92/1/4-18).

Figure 3.6 Parc de la Villette Bioclamatic facades.

Figure 3.7 Sprung suspending components of Parc de la Villette Bioclamatic facades.

Metal casting process

There are a wide range of methods of producing metal casting some of which are more appropriate to the building industry that others. The primary types of castings are:

- sand casting
- lost wax or investment casting
- lost foam
- die casting.

The selection of the casting process is dependent on the component size and form, quantity required, and quality of finish. Some very specialized casting techniques have been developed to match the requirement of particular machine components, for example spun thin wall casting. It should be noted that foundries specialize in particular metals as well as processes.

Sand casting

A pattern is formed, which is a positive of the finished component and incorporates the feeders and risers. The pattern is usually in timber for small quantities, but if larger numbers are required metal or resin patterns are used. The skill of the foundry is to locate the feeders, gates, risers and reservoirs, known as the method, to achieve a good flow of molten metal into the mould. Each metal type and alloy has a different shrinkage rate, which has to be allowed for in the sizing of the pattern. Therefore, if in the design development it is necessary to change the metal specified, for example from stainless steel to aluminium, it is not possible to use the same pattern. Many foundries now use flow analysis software related to CAD models to inform the sizing of the pattern and the location of the feeders. The pattern is normally formed in two halves, each is placed in a moulding box and surrounded by stabilized sand. Sand casting typically have a rough surface finish and interface areas require machining to provide smooth and close tolerance.

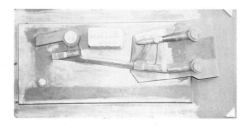

Figure 3.8 Timber pattern of the sand casting for the Thames Water Tower.

The means of stabilizing the sand has been developed to aid castablity and improve surface finish. These include clay bonded sand, sodium silca bonded sand, resin bonded sand, and vacuum moulding. Clay bonded sand consists of quartz sand, bentonite and water as a binder. The advantage of this mix is that it can be strengthened by packing or pressing around the pattern in the moulding box. Resin bonded sand is a development derived from clay bonded sand. Quartz sand is mixed with resin, such as polyurethane and a catalyst, and the sand is often compacted by vibration. The disadvantage of this process, to the foundry, is that

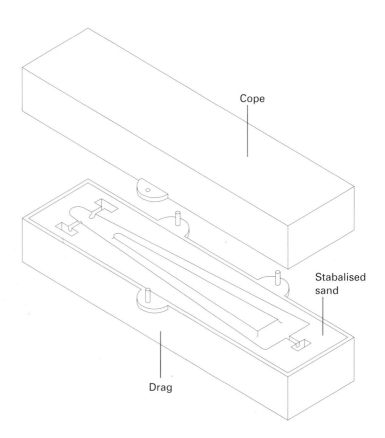

Figure 3.9 Diagram for the sand box of the screen/barrier bronze sand castings for Regional Rail.

the mould is not strong enough until the resin has hardened, thus delaying the removal of the pattern and the casting of the components. Sodium silica sand is hardened by a chemical reaction caused by the introduction of CO_2. Vacuum moulding was developed in the early 1970s; its advantage is that loose sand can be used without a binder and a good cast surface can be obtained.

In all forms of casting the exposed feeders have to be removed by grinding. The specifier may also require the die lines to be similarly removed. The hand finishing of the casting is known as fettling. The design of the cast form can aid the fettling processes and therefore an early interaction with the foundry is essential in the design of the casting. For example, it may be possible to locate the feeders within the casting, such as the tubular nodes of the primary structure of the Parc de la Villette.

Sand castings are appropriate for small runs and very large castings, offering considerable freedom in design, dimension and weight. The typical cost of a pattern for a casting approximately 1000 mm height and a section weight of 24 kg is under £600. Lead time is dependent on many factors including design development and activity level of the foundry; typically a lead time 4–6 weeks should be allowed from approved shop drawings.

Lost wax

This is a very ancient process, possibly as old as civilization itself. The patterns were made of beeswax, packed with clay, dried in the sun and fired causing the wax to melt, leaving a mould into which the metal could be poured. After cooling the mould was broken away and the cast object cleaned. The current method is basically unchanged. However, wax patterns are made with the use of dies and the clay replaced by sand-based ceramics. The wax is injection moulded into aluminium dies, which are typically formed by spark erosion, a means of removing the metal to form the negative profile, which is then polished. Moving parts to produce insets and undercuts are made in brass. The dies themselves can be objects of great beauty. They are also extremely durable and capable of producing a high number of patterns.

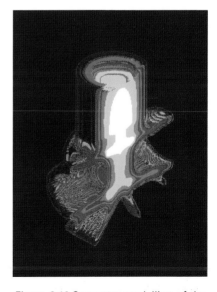

Figure 3.10 Computer modelling of the solidification process in a sand casting.

71

(a)

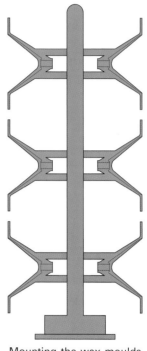

Mounting the wax moulds
on the 'tree' or method   (c)

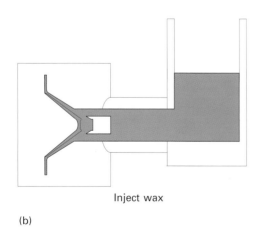

Inject wax

(b)

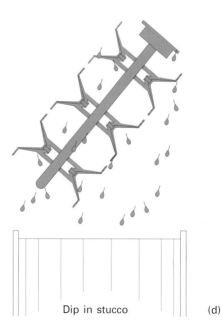

Dip in stucco   (d)

Figure 3.11(a–j) Lost wax or investment casting
for East Croydon Station roof glazing.

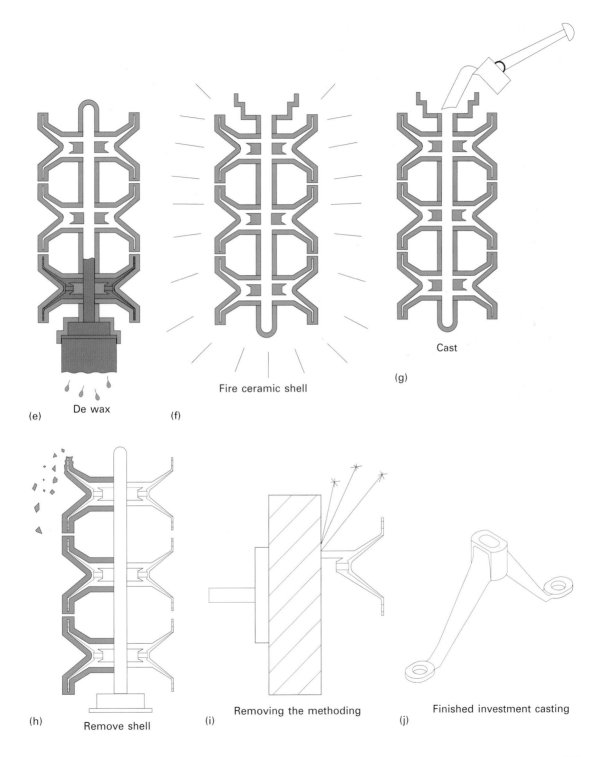

(e) De wax (f) Fire ceramic shell (g) Cast

(h) Remove shell (i) Removing the methoding (j) Finished investment casting

Figure 3.12 Lost wax tree being coated in ceramic slurry at MBC.

Figure 3.13 Molten metal being poured into ceramic lost wax shells at MBC.

The wax patterns are mounted on to a feeder riser or tree made of recycled wax. This is then coated in ceramic slurry, based on zircon (processed Australian beach sand). The ceramic shell is fired and the wax is lost; it melts away and is recycled.

Lost wax produces castings with a high dimensional accuracy and a good surface finish. Lost wax is appropriate for repeats over 100. The as-cast surface roughness is of the order of 4 µm and machining of interface components is not required. Feeder ports still need to be fettled, cut off, and dressed unless discretely located.

The dies to form a lost wax casting are relatively expensive, typically between £2000 and £5000, and castings can be formed up to 100 kg with a maximum dimension of 1000 mm. Maximum sizes vary from

Figure 3.14 Lost wax stainless steel castings of East Croydon Station wall glazing system.

foundry to foundry; one determinant is the relative fragility of the wax pattern. BSA (now MBC) who produced the stainless steel castings for the glazing system of East Croydon station, currently quote a lead time of 9 weeks from approved die drawings, depending on the complexity of the casting.

Lost foam

Established in the 1950s, this technique has developed considerably in the last 10 years. To match the need to reduce the size and weight of car engines, injected moulded polystyrene is now extensively used to produce compact engine components. The pattern can be made of elements that are glued together. Foam patterns can be used in sand casting techniques. For example, the pattern is located in vibrated loose quartz sand and the

Figure 3.15 Lost wax stainless steel castings support the clear toughened glass of East Croydon Station.

mould is stabilized by means of a vacuum. The molten metal is poured onto the polystyrene pattern, which vaporizes, and the mould is filled. Foam patterns can also be used in ceramic shells similar to the lost wax process and there are a number of patented techniques, such as Replicast. A lost foam process was considered for the cast arms of East Croydon Station, at a stage when it was thought that they might be too large to be formed as wax patterns.

Lost foam minimizes finishing, as the pattern can be in one piece, it provides a relatively good surfaces finish and good dimensional accuracy. It is possible to make complex moulds and produce prototypes by using machined polystyrene. Lead times for lost foam are similar to lost wax unless machined polystyrene is used.

Die casting

Die casting is appropriate for metals with a lower melting point than steel, as the metal is poured into a steel mould. The moulds are thus very expensive and this

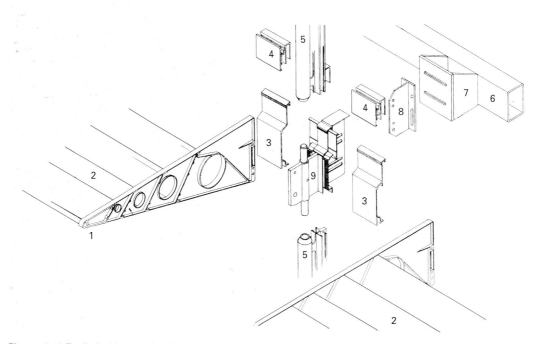

Figure 3.16 Exploded isometric of *brise soleil* of the Hong and Shanghai Bank (drawn by Cupples).
1. Die cast aluminium support bracket; 1. Extruded aluminium fins; 2. Extruded aluminium fascia; 3. Extruded aluminium horizontal glazing channel; 4. Mullion – extruded aluminium with cast aluminium conical end pieces; 5. Perimeter steel RHS fixed back to slab; 6. Steel bracket; 7. Adjustable steel anchor tee; 8. Cast and extruded aluminium fixing assembly with stainless steel spigot.

process is predominantly used to produce accurate machine parts. It is a high speed, high volume application of casting technology. A typical construction application is the treads of an escalator. This demonstrates the precision and complexity of form that can be achieved by using a die casting. However, the die costs are relatively high and therefore a repeat of 2500 is typically necessary. The cast brackets which support the *brise soleil* of the Hong and Shanghai Bank by Foster Associates (Foster & Partners) is an exemplary use of an aluminium die casting, producing a finely engineered and dynamic component, which is a vital part of the architecture of the Bank. With 4000 brackets in the complete façade, a die casting was an eminently appropriate method of production.

Figure 3.17 Exterior detail of the Hong and Shanghai Bank showing the die cast *brise soleil*.

Finishes

There is an incredible diversity of finishes available on cast components; some enhance the metallic qualities whereas others bury it under a plastic coating. It is interesting to contrast the characteristic bronze quality of the patinated gun metal castings of Bracken House (which were cast by Sweetmore and patinated by Capsco) with the cast aluminium brackets used on the refurbished Circle Line trains (by Precision-Cast Components Ltd.), which are polyester coated and could be mistaken for plastic components.

The need for a good quality finish when the casting is to be an exposed component of the architecture, needs to be communicated to the foundry at the earliest possible stage. There is a clear division in the foundry industry, which is dependent on the foundry background. Foundries that are established to manufacture machine components

Figure 3.18 Patinated gun metal castings of Bracken House.

Figure 3.19 Barry Flanagan's 'Large Leaping Hare' 1982, bronze and steel – edition of four plus three artist's casts, 2820 × 2820 × 1120 mm (courtesy of Barry Flanagan and Waddington Gallery).

are often unfamiliar with the need for a careful control of the surface finish. Whereas foundries that regularly produce fine art castings, are familiar with the need for a high quality finish. This split tends to be material based, with aluminium and steel used predominantly for mechanical components and bronze for sculptures. It is interesting to note that Sweetmore regularly cast Barry Flanagan's Hares.

All castings require finishing to remove mould residue. Hand polishing, as used for casting yacht components, is an expensive option, although necessary where there is a high corrosion risk, such as the contained and damp environment of the Thames Water Tower. There is a wide range of finishes available using blasting techniques, from grit blasting to shot blasting and they often are used in combination. The size and sharpness of the projectile and pressure used are important, and the final finish should be agreed via samples. On stainless steel castings that are to be shot blasted, it is critical that clean stainless steel shot is used or apparent rusting will occur as a result of non-stainless steel residue. Unseen cast components that need to be de-burred are often tumbled with glass beads. Electropolishing, as used on the pin-jointed castings of Waterloo International Terminal, provides a reliable silvery finish; however, it tends to disguise the stainless steel quality of the casting itself. Anodizing is not recommended for aluminium castings, if a match to an anodized extrusion is required, as the presence of silica in the casting turns 'natural' anodizing dark grey.

Stabilized aluminium foam

In the 1990s a new metallurgic option was developed for lightweight metal components. Using a continuous casting process, CYMT Ontario produced closed cell foam aluminium. This process, developed by Alcan International, enables them to produce aluminium foam which is only 2.5% aluminium with a bulk density of only 68 kg/m³ compared to 2760 kg/m² for aluminium itself. A section held in your hand weighs significantly less than a chocolate 'Aero' bar it resembles. The thermal conductivity of 2.5% aluminium foam is 0.028 W/m°C, which compares to 0.037 W/m°C for mineral wool insulation with a density of 24 kg/m². It is possible to produce aluminium foam in a range of bulk densities from 20% to 2.5%. The density is controlled by the average cell size and average wall thickness. At 20% the average cell size is 3 mm with an average wall thickness of 86 µm; at 6% this is 9 mm and 50 µm, respectively.

Stabilized aluminium foam can be used as a monolithic panel on its own or as a core of a laminated composite. The skins of a monolithic panel can be coated or finished as a 'solid' aluminium composite (see Chapter 5). Stabilized aluminium foam can potentially be cast to form 3D components using the casting techniques in this chapter.

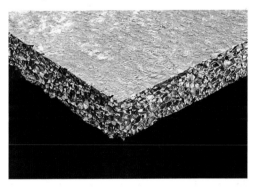

Figure 3.20 Cross-section of stabilized aluminium foam.

Design by co-operation

To develop a cast component it is necessary not only to have a clear understanding of the processes available, but it is also essential to establish a close working relationship with a foundry. Only some foundries provide a full design service. This, however, does not fit well into the standard commercial modes of procurement, in the building industry, or the automotive manufacture. The managing director of a Dutch foundry Herumetal b.v., Adriaan Hendrix, has described the pre-tender process as 'living in the land of the cannibals'. Competitive tendering can result in the ideas and information of the foundry, the co-designer's of the component, being used in the product supplied by a competitor who is finally awarded the order. It is possible to avoid this by appointing a foundry, which has a design capability, to design and prototype the casting at an agreed cost.

To specify castings an architect or engineer needs to identify the requirement early in the design process or to introduce sufficient flexibility in the mode of procurement to accommodate the proposal to cast a given component. There is the need to carefully research the finish and testing requirement, for incorporation into the specification, preferably a performance specification. A form of contract that creates the closest possible links between the architect/engineer and the subcontractor is desirable.

Castings are often sourced as part as of a larger subcontract, and the use of castings can be proposed by the subcontractor. For example, Tubeworkers based on their experience on the Renault Centre, Swindon (Foster Associates), proposed the use of cast nodes on Victoria Plaza Canopy (Heery Architects & Engineers) for speed and accuracy, although they were designed as fabrications; they still look like fabrications as there was no time in the fast track programme to revise their form. One of the first use of castings to support a toughened glass assembly in the UK was 111 Lotts Road, built in 1988 and designed by Goldstein Ween, with engineers Price and Myers. The advantages of castings were proposed by the steelwork subcontractor, Non-Corrosive Metal Products. These aluminium bronze castings (AB2 to BS 1400, 1985) were produced by Woodcock and Booth.

On Waterloo International Terminal by Nicholas Grimshaw, the paired

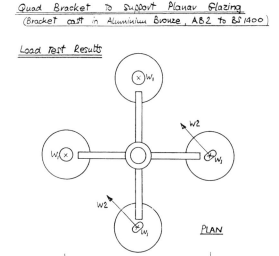

Quad Bracket to Support Planar Glazing
(Bracket cast in Aluminium Bronze, AB2 to BS 1400)

Load Test Results

PLAN

SIDE ELEVATION

Loads and Deflections.
Characteristic (Working) Loads were :- W_1 = 1·03 KN on each leg ; W_2 = 1·1 KN on each of two legs. The two loadcases were tested separately. Each was taken to well over 5 times characteristic Load. Deflections were negligible (< 1·0mm @ 2½ x W).

Figure 3.21 Aluminium bronze castings at Lotts Road.

pin-jointed castings used to support the under-slung glazing were proposed and designed by Briggs Amasco Curtain Walling Ltd. Grimshaw tendered the package with machined aluminium components.

The work of Grimshaw demonstrates some of the potential of the use of castings in contemporary architecture. However, Martin Wood, a project architect on Western Morning News points to the dilemma of the need to avoid nominating a subcontractor, for contractual reasons; the sourcing of the cast component is taken out of the architect's control and the package subcontractor will seek the lowest possible price. This emphasizes the need for a detailed and thorough specification.

Figure 3.22 Pin-jointed lost wax castings of the external glazing at Waterloo International Terminal.

Figure 3.23 Timber patterns of the sand castings at Waterloo International Terminal, which form the primary structural nodes.

Key point points to be determined in the specification are:

• base metal and alloy
• casting method
• critical tolerances and interfaces

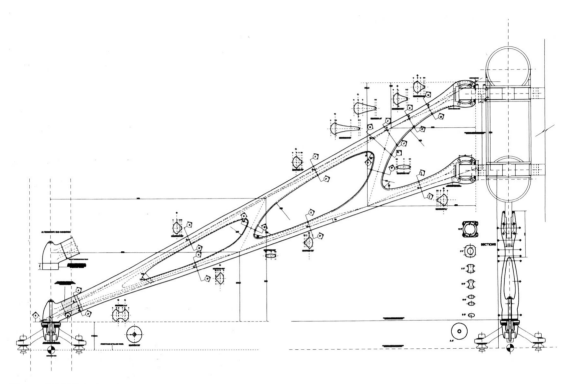

Figure 3.24 Nicholas Grimshaw and Partners' drawing of the spheroidal graphite castings of Western Morning News.

- location of feeders
- surface finish
- National, European or International Standards
- QA procedures including testing requirements.

An important criteria in the selection of an alloy is whether the casting is to be mechanically fixed or needs to be welded into an overall assembly? Only a limited number of casting grade metals can be welded.

Quality control and testing

The integrity of a cast component is critical to its long-term ability to sustain stress. Therefore the need for quality control and testing is clearly understood by a progressive foundry. Many quality assurance systems were set up as a necessity of aerospace or defence procurement, often on an international basis.

MBC for example are registered to BS EN ISO 9002 (formerly BS 5750 Part 2), a quality system for use when conformity to an established design is required. The specific means of inspecting and testing a casting is dependent on the proposed alloy. It should be agreed with the foundry and incorporated into the specification.

Paul Craddock of Ove Arup & Partner, who organized the testing of the Bracken House Gunmetal Castings (LG4 to BS 1400), noted that the presence of lead in a copper alloy made the casting very difficult to radiograph. Casting with a course grain structure cannot be tested ultrasonically, therefore some stainless steel castings are also difficult to test by this means. The castings on Bracken House were therefore tested by a destructive test method on a representative sample of castings. Each was sawn into cross-sections and visually inspected for voids.

It is also important to decide whether traceability is required, where each batch or melt is numbered and stamped into the casting. This is essential in aerospace applications and will be a necessary part of the QA procedure for highly stressed castings use in a building structure.

Fusion

Foundries continue to seek improvements in technique, and there could be an interesting fusion of ceramic, plastic and metal technologies in the near future. Flexible manufacturing techniques are becoming the norm within batch-produced products and castings are an excellent example of the application of industrial batch production to the construction of high quality modern architecture.

Brookes Stacey Randall, with engineers Price & Myers, developed a set of bronze sand castings for a project to refurbish three British Rail stations. These are used as multifunctional building components; the wishbone casting supports queuing systems and glazed screens. The repeat of this casting, manufactured

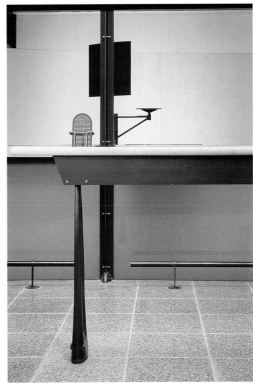

Figure 3.25 Bronze sand castings supporting the queuing barrier of Regional Rail fit out.

Figure 3.26 Enschede Bus Station glazing supported by aluminium bronze sand castings. (Architect IAA-Bookes Stacey Randall)

by Henshaw, is under 30. These castings demonstrate that it is possible and beneficial to use castings on a project with a short lead time and a modest budget. They were designed in 3 weeks; the first pattern was inspected at the foundry 2 weeks after placement of the order and a fully finish sample was supplied within a further 2 weeks. The casting process is a means of uniting function, economy and elegance in a building component.

Further information

BS 3100 (1991)	Specification for steel castings for general engineering purposes
BS 3923	Methods for ultrasonic examination of welds
BS 4570 (1985)	Specification for fusion welding of steel castings
BS 5135 (1984)	Specification for arc welding of carbon and carbon manganese steels
BS 6072 (1986)	Method for magnetic particle flaw detection
BS 6208 (1990)	Method for ultrasonic testing of ferritic steel casting including quality levels

BS 6615 (1996)	Specification for dimensional tolerances for metal and metal alloy castings
BS EN 288	Specification and approval of welding procedures for metallic materials
BS EN 571	Non-destructive testing. Penetrant testing
BS EN 970 (1997)	Non-destructive examination of fusion welds. Visual examination
BS EN 1559	Founding. Technical conditions of delivery
BS EN 1560 (1997)	Founding. Designation system for cast iron
BS EN 1561 (1997)	Founding. Grey cast irons
BS EN 1562 (1997)	Founding. Malleable cast irons
BS EN 1563 (1997)	Founding. Spheroidal graphite cast iron
BS EN 1564 (1997)	Founding. Austempered ductile cast iron
BS EN 1982 (1999)	Copper and copper alloy. Ingots and castings
BS EN10213 (1996)	Technical delivery conditions for steel castings for pressure purpose
ASTM E94 (1992)	Guide to radiographic testing
ASTM A802 (1989)	Standard practice for steel castings, textures and discontinuities, surface acceptance standards, visual examination
ASTM E186 (1991)	Reference radiographs for heavy walled (50–115 mm) steel castings
ASTM E280 (1991)	Reference radiographs for heavy walled (115–300 mm) steel castings
ASTM E446 (1991)	Reference radiographs for steel castings up to 50 mm in thickness
ANSI/AWS D (11.2.89)	Guide for welding iron castings
DIN 1690–2 (1985)	Technical delivery conditions for castings made of metallic materials.
MSS-SP-551985 (R'90)	Quality standard for steel castings for valves, flanges and fittings and other pipe components – Visual methods.

References and further reading

Badoo, N. (1996). *Castings in Construction.* SCI P-172
Dutton, H. and Wernick, J. (1992). Structural glass designs from La Villette – Paris and after. In *The Glass Envelope* (Eekhout, M., ed.). Technische Universiteit Delft.
Stacey, M. (1992). *Application of Metal Castings in Contemporary Architecture.* Technische Universiteit Delft

4

Sheet Metal Forming

'When a metal component is being intelligently designed many factors are taken into account: the cost of the finished article, its strength, reliability in service, and appearance. Often the facilities and skill of the manufacture cause one or other process to be selected' (Alexander and Street, 1976).

All the processes for forming sheet metal are dependent on the ductility of the chosen metal or its alloy. If a metal is pre-finished with a polymeric coating, for example, the capability of the finish withstanding the forming process also needs to be considered. There are four basic methods of forming sheet metal into components:

- roll forming
- press brake
- hand forming
- pressing or stamping.

Table 4.1 Material properties of copper

Property	Value
Density	8960 kg/m^3
Young's modulus	128 kN/mm^2
Thermal conductivity	393 W/m°C
Co-efficient of thermal expansion	1.65×10^{-5} per °C
Corrosion resistance	Excellent
Melting point	1083°C
Recyclability	Excellent
Primary embodied energy[*]	986 GJ/m^3

*Data supplied by BRE

Roll forming

Profiled sheet cladding or roofing are very familiar linear building components. However, the process and its constraints remain unfamiliar to many architects. Most roll formers purchase the sheet metal in coil or pre-cut blanks. Often this is pre-finished steel coated in Plastisol or PVF[2] or pre-patinated metal, such as copper. The aim of roll forming is to produce a rigid component from a thin sheet metal by developing a cross-section of sufficient depth for the required span. The profile is formed by the progressive development of the shape by roll form tools (see Figure 4.1).

It is essential that the final form is developed progressively in stages. A tool to develop an apparently simple square edge will have eight stages. If a desired form is produced in too few stages, too abruptly, the form will lack precision. All roll forming is subject to flaring where the ends of the sheet, say a panel skin, will be wider at the two ends than the middle. This is the result of release of tension at the end of the profile. If a sheet is not feed through square to the tool, residual stress will result in the sheet not being flat, unacceptable in the face of panel, for example. This is known by the literal metaphor: crabbing.

Figure 4.1 Roll forming the edges of a metal sheet to form the face of a metal composite panel.

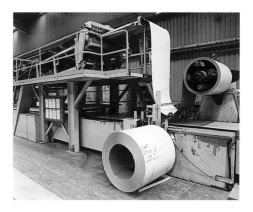

Figure 4.2 Decoiling steel sheet.

One constraint on roll-formed sheet components is the availability and size of sheet material; a roll of 1.6 mm thick steel sheet is typically 430 m long. The constraint is primarily the width; a typical maximum is 1250 mm depending on the substrate and additional process required, although 1500 mm wide sheet is available in some metals. It is important to remember the width of the final product is a result of the developed form. Essentially any stretching of the metal is minor and can be negated; the width is a resultant of the surface length of the profile.

Standing seam roofs

Hoogovens patented its Kal Zip standing seam roof in the 1960s, which has now lapsed. It is, therefore, a tried and tested product, but Hoogovens are exposed to competitive pressure and imitation. Hoogovens (now Corus following its 1999 merger with British Steel) aim to stay ahead through a combination of innovation and service. Although its activities are enriched by R&D in the overall Hoogovens Group, for example alloys developed for aircraft bodies are now used for standing seam roofs, the majority of developments are market-driven and CAD modelling is clearly stimulating the exploration of form in construction. Hoogovens now provide 3D modelling on Microstation as a design development service for architects. An aluminium standing seam roof sheet can be formed to a 30–40 m radius on site without distortion and the need for pre-curving. The minimum radius is dependent on the gauge specified. Hoogovens can produce curved sheet to a radius as tight as 1.5 m without crimping.

Hoogovens has also been able to produce tapered sheets since the early 1990s, thus avoiding cutting and welding sheets or large hip flashings. BDP, for the replacement roof of the Number One Court at Wimbledon, conceived of a 'grid shell' clad in a tapered and curved sheet to form a smooth toroidal roof. To achieve this combination of tapering and curving Hoogovens invested £250 000 in machinery and development during 1996. The roof of Number One Court is

Figure 4.3 Tapered aluminium sheets forming the smooth toroidal of Wimbledon Number One Court (architect BDP).

now complete and the equipment is already being reused on other projects and providing a positive return for Hoogovens investment.

Seventy-five percent of projects completed by Hoogovens in 1996 were 'self-finished' as this specification offers lower maintenance and higher durability than post-coated sheet. Although described as 'self-finished' the sheet is formed of two aluminium alloys rolled together. The outer layer or 'Kal Alloy' weathers to a consistent grey colour forming a protective oxide coating and avoiding the sugary appearance of exposed mill-finished aluminium. The Agreement Certificate for Kal Zip states a durability for the product in excess of 40 years. This is currently under review and Hoogovens expect this to be increased, based on regular testing of a project in Hamburg docks installed over 30 years ago.

At the Scottish Exhibition and Conference Centre in Glasgow, Foster & Partners selected a standing seam aluminium roof to clad the eight shells, for is economy, durability, and its self-finished metallic appearance. Robin Partington of Foster & Partners described the essential volumes of the auditorium as being 'shrunk-wrapped in aluminium'. The void between the internal concrete walls and the shell forms dynamic horizontal circulation and meeting spaces.

Figure 4.4 The Scottish Exhibition and Conference Centre in Glasgow described by the Project Director as 'shrunk wrapped in aluminium'. (Architect Foster and Partners)

This project demonstrates that 3D CAD modelling can facilitate freedom in design intent and its resolution. The shape of the roof is derived from cylindrical forms of a consistent radius, with the standing seam running parallel to the radius. The aluminium standing seam roof was supplied by Hoogovens and installed by Briggs Major Projects.

Welding

Aluminium should no longer be considered as 'difficult' to weld. The skin and structure of the Networker 465 commuter train is formed from welded sheet aluminium to form a smooth outer profile and a monocoque construction. Similarly, the hulls of the Sea Cat catamaran are formed of welded aluminium.

Figure 4.5 Networker 465.

The TIG or Tungsten Inert Arc welding process was invented in the 1940s. In this process an arc is struck between a non-combustible tungsten electrode and the work piece, with filler rod being fed independently. Fluxes are unnecessary and oxidization is prevented by a shield of inert gas that envelops the weld area.

The techniques of welding developed in the factory or fabricating yard can now be reliably applied to site conditions. The need to form weather-tight and durable penetrations in aluminium standing seam roofs has led firms like Melvyn Rowberry Welding Services, to develop site welding techniques using portable equipment based in a modified van. TIG welding be carried out on aluminium sheets as thin as 0.5 mm and at a range of 200 m from the van.

Although the form of the Scottish Exhibition and Conference Centre was designed to avoid penetrations through the roof, they are all located in the slot between shells. Welding of the aluminium has been specified for a number of reasons.

- It proved to be more economical to weld sheets together rather than roll form on site. Even allowing for the constraint of the weather, work started on site in the autumn of 1996.
- Welded details have been used to control thermal movement, for example the ridge is 'locked off' and movement accommodated at the base and leading edge.

Briggs, the installers, carried out a number of mock-ups of the roof assembly for the Scottish Exhibition and Conference Centre in a Glasgow warehouse and found that they were to prove vital to the successful installation. They also chose to weld the flashing on the interface to the glass panels to avoid difficulties generated by the radial geometry. Although some local distortion was noted around

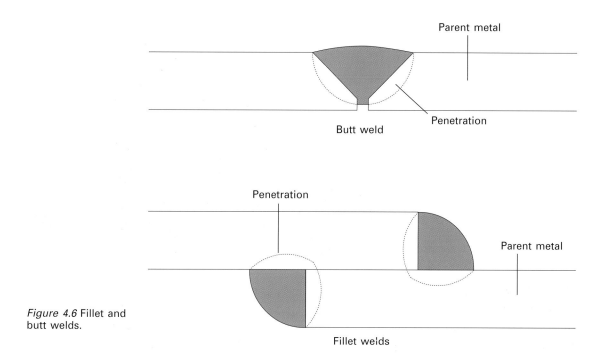

Figure 4.6 Fillet and butt welds.

the welded details, Robin Partington stated this was not an problem on a roof of this scale.

Press brake

One way of avoiding flaring in forming a sheet component such as a metal tray is to use a press brake. The metal is formed by the action of the upper press tool into the bed or lower tool of the press. The pressure necessary is dependent on the gauge, or thickness, of the metal. As the force is applied as a uniformly distributed load over the length of the section an even fold results, thus avoiding flaring. For a square section it is a one-stage process. A constraint of a press brake is the length of the press, typically 3–4 m, although presses up to 12 m can be found in Europe. It is possible to use two press brakes together with staggered tools. Sheet metal up to 10 mm can be press brake, however the associated tolerances typically increase with thickness. Press brakes are inherently flexible with interchangeable top and bottoms tools, tool selection is based on the angle and radius required in the pressing.

The minimum radius at the corner of a 90° uncoated press-braked section is a function of the thickness of the metal, where internal radius equals the thickness

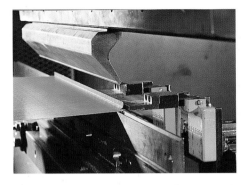

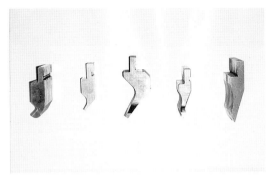

Figure 4.7 Press braking a 90° edge; a second 90° is about to be formed (photograph courtesy of **ame**).

Figure 4.8 A range of top tools removed from a press brake demonstrating the flexibility of this method of forming sheet metal.

of the metal (see Figure 4.9). For a pre-coated metal the radius should not exceed the stretch ability of the coating (see Figure 4.10). When press braking aluminium it is essential that the alloy and work hardening of the sheet are carefully controlled. If an inappropriate alloy is used, either the final component will not be stiff enough or stretch cracking and/or brittle failure will occur, thus a component will either not function correctly, look unsightly, or premature failure will result.

In designing a press-braked component it is essential that there is sufficient room for the tool to be withdrawn. This has lead to the development of swan-neck tools, which allow deep channel sections to be formed. If a narrow channel section is required it may be necessary to make the vertical side asymmetrical in height, to enable the component to be removed from the tool (see Figure 4.11). It is possible to press-brake smooth curved sections, as demonstrated by the press braked and then anodized aluminium gutter of East Croydon Station (architect Brookes Stacey Randall, produced by Majors of Croydon). The details of the restored roof of Nash's pavilion at Brighton used the same production method. The constructional aesthetic is not governed by the technology.

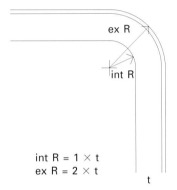

$$int\ R = 1 \times t$$
$$ex\ R = 2 \times t$$

Figure 4.9 Recommended minimum radius for press-braking a coil-coated metal: HPS200 (PVC).

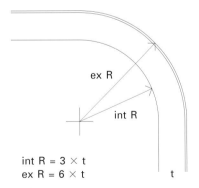

$$int\ R = 3 \times t$$
$$ex\ R = 6 \times t$$

Figure 4.10 Recommended minimum radius for press-braking a coil-coated metal: PVF^2.

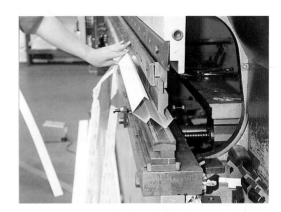

Figure 4.11 It is essential to design for the removal of the press tool.

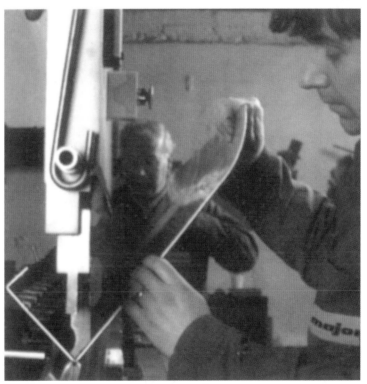

Figure 4.12 Aluminium gutter of East Croydon Station being press braked by Majors of Croydon.

In producing a smooth curve it is essential that the section is pressed in small increments, otherwise telegraphed steps will show. This process can be aided by the use of a computer-controlled press brake. The presence of telegraphed lines can also be a function of thickness. Curved column casings with folded fixing flanges are an example of a component that could only be press braked as it would be impossible to design a roll-forming tool through which the sheet travel.

Roll forming and press braking produce linear components. If a rotated geometry in metal is desired, or required, a spinning should be considered.

Spinning

The spinning process is probably familiar from aluminium light fittings. As a forming method it is equally appropriate for steel and stainless steel. Figure 4.13 shows the 1800 mm diameter spun stainless steel bath designed by Brookes Stacey Randall for the Art House, which is based on a standard stainless steel spinning used in a milk tanker. This spinning process starts with a flat sheet of the chosen metal which is rotated at speed and formed over a hardwood or steel tool. It is also possible to form thin-walled rotated forms using spun castings.

Figure 4.13 The 1800 mm diameter spun stainless steel bath designed by Brookes Stacey Randall, for the Art House.

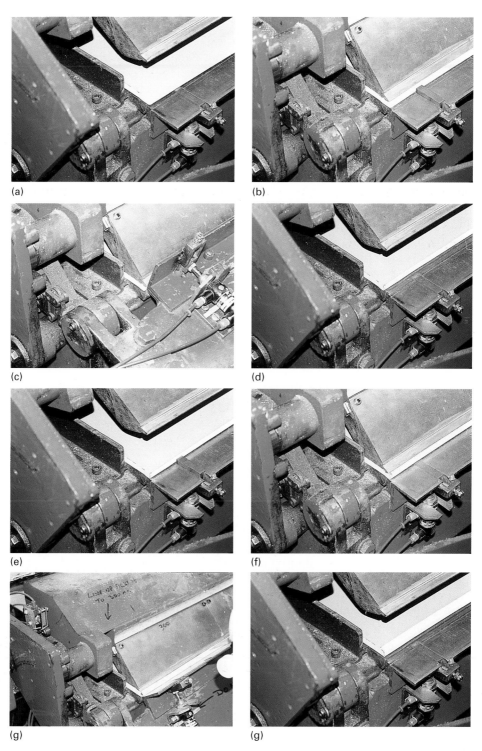

(a)

(b)

(c)

(d)

(e)

(f)

(g)

(g)

Figure 4.14
(a–h) The eight
stages of
forming two
90° returns on
a metal sheet
cladding 'skin'
or panel face.

Box folder

A box folder is an alternative to a press brake and is used when the components always have a rectilinear form. As the name suggests, metal boxes are required. Figure 4.14(a–h) shows the eight stages of forming two 90° returns on a metal sheet cladding 'skin' or panel face. The other two edges shown have been roll formed. This is a front or rear sheet of a composite cladding panel being produced by **ame**. The dimensions of the folds can be varied by the position of the stops, which can be computer controlled.

If a dedicated fold is required when forming a metal component in a large scale production run, such as a filing cabinet, a Salvagnini bender represents an alternative to a press brake. These are numerically-controlled, providing automatic yet flexible production of sheet panel components. A Salvagnini bender is used by Bisely to produce is steel filing cabinets. The typical capabilities of a Salvagnini bender (P4-3816) are:

Maximum length of sheet on entry, 3995 mm
Maximum width of sheet on entry, 1500 mm
Maximum bending length, 3850 mm
Maximum bending height, 160 mm
Minimum sheet thickness, 0.5 mm
Steel maximum sheet thickness, 1 mm
Stainless steel maximum sheet thickness, 0.6 mm
Aluminium maximum sheet thickness, 1 mm.

Sheet Metal and Hand Forming

The availability of metal forming machinery has not totally displaced site-formed metal cladding and roofing. Approximately 30 years ago sheet metal would have been delivered to site as flat sheet and weatherproof lapped junctions formed primarily with a wooden mallet. This skilled site activity was carried out traditionally by plumbers. The metal used in formed or lapped cladding is usually self-finished and includes lead, zinc, copper, and stainless steel. Apart from lead, which is too soft, zinc and copper sheet is now delivered to site as roll-formed sheet, or roll formed on site using a mobile roll-forming tool, such as Profimat SPA. The sealing of the standing seal if usually carried out by mobile former. For zinc it is critical that the air temperature is over 10°C to ensure that the zinc remains ductile. This can be overcome by the use of direct-acting warm air fans. Only the difficult or complex end details or junctions are now hand formed.

Figure 4.15 Titanium cladding of the Guggenheim Museum Bilbo (architect Frank Gery).

For the Guggenheim Museum Bilbo, Frank Gery was able to show that in the context of a regional arts building, titanium was cost effective. The complex forms of the galley are clad in sheets 750 × 1300 mm, which are only 0.38 mm thick. Titanium is a very hard metal and the sheets were rolled in the USA by Timet. The contract for supply and fixing of this shimmering cladding was under-taken by P.M. Umaran. Sources of design guidance on formed sheet metal roofing and cladding include the Lead Sheet Association, the Copper Development Association, and Applications in Architecture by Rheinzink.

Zinc

When used to form standing seam roofs and wall cladding zinc is used as an alloy with titanium and copper; however, it is 99.995% zinc. It is manufactured in accordance with EN501201. Zinc offers a very high level of durability if it is correctly installed. Zinc patinates in a number of stages. First, oxygen in the air forms zinc oxide on the surface. This in turn reacts with water, rain, or humidity, which leads to the formation of zinc hydroxide, which then reacts with CO_2 to form a dense, firmly adhering layer of zinc carbonate. It is zinc carbonate that forms the characteristic blue grey patina on zinc, and it is the presence of this patina that makes zinc a very durable cladding or roofing material. Tests undertaken for Rheinzink in the Ruhr, an industrial region of Germany, showed that these zinc roofs have a minimum life expectancy of 80–100 years.

Both Sogem and Rheinzink offer pre-patinated zinc if a pre-weathered and visually unchanging finish is required. Zinc can be lacquered to a finish comparable with polyester powder coating. Unlike copper, zinc presents little problem in terms of staining of other materials. The compatibility of other materials in the build-up of a roof using zinc needs to be considered. For example, phenolics in plywood can cause accelerated pit corrosion. Bitumen subject to UV radiation and weather can result in bituminous waste products that will cause zinc to corrode. In preparing assembly details the galvanic potential of zinc should also be considered. Direct contact with aluminium is not a problem; see Professor Witt's (1997) paper, 'The corrosive behaviour of aluminium in contact with zinc in building construction'. However, contact with copper should be avoided at all times.

Table 4.2 Sheet metal gauge thicknesses

Gauge	Inches	mm
1	0.30	7.6
2	0.28	7.0
3	0.25	6.4
4	0.23	5.9
5	0.21	5.4
6	0.19	4.9
7	0.18	4.5
8	0.16	4.1
9	0.14	3.7
10	0.13	3.3
11	0.12	2.9
12	0.10	2.6
13	0.09	2.3
14	0.08	2.0
15	0.07	1.8
16	0.064	1.63
17	0.056	1.42
18	0.048	1.22
19	0.040	1.02
20	0.036	0.91
21	0.032	0.81
22	0.028	0.71
23	0.024	0.61
24	0.022	0.56
25	0.020	0.51
26	0.018	0.46
27	0.016	0.42
28	0.015	0.38
29	0.014	0.35
30	0.012	0.31
31	0.012	0.29
32	0.011	0.27

As is the case with all metal roofs, the potential corrosion of the under surface should be considered. Either a stable patina is encouraged to form by the use of a ventilated roof, or a warm roof should be specified. In the latter, it is critical that internal humidity is prevented from reaching the underside of the zinc sheeting, thus a high performance vapour check layer is required. Water entrapped in the construction

Figure 4.16 Zinc cladding of Hogeschool Enschede (architect Harry Abels of IAA-Brookes Stacey Randall).

also needs to be considered. One successful form of zinc sheet warm roof uses Foamglas insulation beaded in bitumen. If a ventilated assembly is selected, clear design guidance is available on the necessary height of the ventilated space, which is dependent on pitch or angle of application. The detailing of ventilation at eaves and ridges needs to be consistent and the ventilation of particular areas, such as dormer roof lights, requires particular consideration. For roofs with a pitch below 10°, a ventilated ridge is not usually required.

Examples of published design guidance are listed at the end of this chapter and the leading suppliers of zinc will supply specific design guidance for a potential project.

The other governing consideration in designing with zinc is its relatively high coefficient of thermal expansion. As zinc is a rolled product it has a different lengthways coefficient of thermal expansion, 2.2 mm/m°C compared to the lateral coefficient of thermal expansion, 1.7 mm/m°C.

Copper

Until late in the nineteenth century, copper sheet was produced only in limited sizes. Current production techniques now produce coils of copper of typically 30 m in length. Combined with roll forming and other mechanized forming processes, this has significantly improved its cost effectiveness and has revitalized the use of copper. It now offers a combination of affordability, durability, and depth of colour. A well-detailed copper roof has a life expectancy in excess of 100 years. It is chastening to note that the oldest intact copper roof protects Hildersheim Cathedral and dates from 1280. The copper used in the building envelope is oxygen-free phosphorous deoxidized copper (SF-Cu). The purity is defined by BS EN 1172, which states that the sheet or strip should have a minimum of 99.9% copper.

With a melting point of 1083°C, copper sheet can be joined by soldering, brazing and welding. If welding is used consideration needs to be made of the high thermal conductivity of copper and the formation of oxides, thus TIG welding is particularly appropriate. Fusion between the components is induced by the arc, which burns between the electrode and the work. This is shielded from the atmosphere by an inert gas such as argon.

Untarnished copper when first produced is a golden red colour and on contact with air a film of cupric oxide is formed, which acts as a protective layer. This oxide layer continues to form on the installed copper resulting from the reaction of the copper with water, oxygen, and atmospheric pollutants. This leads to the formation of a generally uniform brown coloration. After an extended period of exposure this will darken to dark brown or anthracite appearance. The oxide layer becomes both thicker and stronger. It is the result of rainwater lying on the surface that weathers this oxide layer to the characteristic green patina. Thus vertical surface and overhangs of mill finish copper will not patina to green and typically remain dark brown. For the roof and hull of the Boat Pavilion Streatly, Brookes Stacey Randall chose to use mill finish cooper. The roof will eventually patinate over time; however, the hull will probably only oxide to a rich brown. The formulation of the green patina is dependent on the location of the building. In industrial and urban areas, copper sulphate predominates, in marine environments copper chloride is dominant, whereas in rural areas copper carbonate is formed. In detailing the roof to wall junctions it is essential to remember that the patina is water soluble and can stain stone or concrete.

Figure 4.17 Boat Pavilion Streatley by Brookes Stacey Randall.

If a green patina is desired from day one, possibly for the repair of an existing patinated roof or to form swathes of colour, as in the B. Braun Factory by James Stirling and Michael Wilford, pre-patinated copper is available. The Braun Factory is clad in TECU pre-patinated copper manufactured by KME. The sheets are pre-patinated in the factory, by a mechanical, chemical and thermal process, which produces a patina that closely resembles the colour performance of an atmospherically-produced patina. The patina will become thicker during exposure on site and the colour will develop depending on local atmospheric conditions. Pre-patinated copper has variability of colour and extended durability which cannot be matched by polyester powder coating, although an initial RAL number match can be achieved as was suggested in one 'value engineering process'.

KME's maximum pre-patinated sheet length is 3000 mm, with a maximum width of 1000 mm and a maximum thickness of 1.5 mm, whereas a mill finish is available in widths up to 1250 mm. If pre-patinated copper is used, particular care is required in handling and detailing so as not to damage the patination. KME advise that minor scratches will 'heal' naturally due to the weathering process. Further than that all normal forming, bending, folding, and seaming techniques can be used without reservation. However, the use of double lock welt is not recommended as it can leave a fold mark, which is unsightly. Similarly, only soft solder joints should be used in components such as gutters as the high temperature associated with hard soldering permanently damages the pre-patina.

Should you wish to avoid the visual variability of mill-finished copper, it is possible to specify pre-oxidized copper that offers a consistent dark brown. If a matt grey finish is desired, the alternatives to zinc include: tin plated copper, terncoated stainless steel or lead.

Figure 4.18 The pre-patinated copper clad loading area of B. Braun Factory by James Stirling and Michael Wilford.

Figure 4.19 Detail of the pre-patinated copper cladding of the B. Braun Factory.

Pressed Cladding

It is possible to form sheet metals by the application of pressure, typically with a two-part steel tool. An example is the cross rib that stiffens Planja 200 sheeting. Steel press tools tend to be expensive and therefore dedicated to a single product. The panel system for Herman Miller Chippenham, design by Nicholas Grimshaw & Partners, and the cladding of the Patera system by Michael Hopkins & Partners, are both pressed steel cladding. The automotive industry extensively uses deep-drawn doubly-curved steel body panels, although there is now significant use of thermoplastic panels, as in the Mercedes A class or aluminium, as in the Audi 8.

In press forming the aim is to stiffen the panel by inducing permanent deformation, and accessing the plasticity of the material, which is a product of its ductility. The limitation of cold forming metals under pressures is their ductility, which leads to the dangers of either brittle failure or wrinkling. This can be overcome by the use of superplastic alloys, which are capable of elongation of up to 1000%, which compares to an elongation of 30–40% for typical steel or aluminium alloy.

Figure 4.20 Pressed steel cladding of Patera system building by Michael Hopkins & Partners.

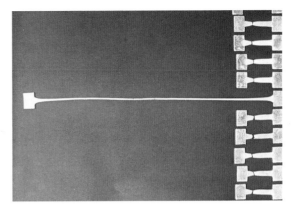

Figure 4.21 Superplastic aluminium on test.

Superplastic alloys

It is possible to produce superplastic alloys of steel, zinc or titanium. However, it is superplastic aluminium that is now extensively used to form aerospace and architectural components. The superplastic quality of an alloy is the product of a fine and stabilized grain structure resulting in high ductility. Superplastic aluminium is appropriate when a doubly curved element or a component with a complex surface is required. The aim is to create stiffness in an otherwise flat component, such as a cladding panel, or to interface with the geometry of other components as in an aero-engine air intake. The rear of the Networker 465/3 commuter train is formed in superplastic aluminium, by Superform of Worcester and California (see Figure 4.5). This doubly curved component has a 3-mm starting gauge of 5083 alloy. It is metal inert gas (MIG) welded onto the aluminium body of the train.

The range of superplastic aluminium alloys available includes: Supral 100 and 150 (2004), Supral 5000 (5251) 5083SPF, 7475SPF, and 8090 SPF. Alloys are selected on the basis of required stiffness and forming method.

The are four primary methods of superplastic forming:

- cavity forming – conventional and drape
- bubble forming
- diaphragm forming
- back pressure forming.

103

Cavity forming

Figure 4.22 illustrates the process. A sheet is preheated and clamped into the press. It is then forced into a cavity moulded by air pressure. The profiled cladding panels of the Sainsbury Supermarket in Camden, London by Nicholas Grimshaw & Partners, were produced by cavity forming. Designers should note that the thickness of the sheet reduces in the 'deepest' parts of the mould. The thickness can be controlled by varying the cycle and speed at which air is blown. A minimum thickness should be specified and the metal deployed, if possible, where it is needed within the component.

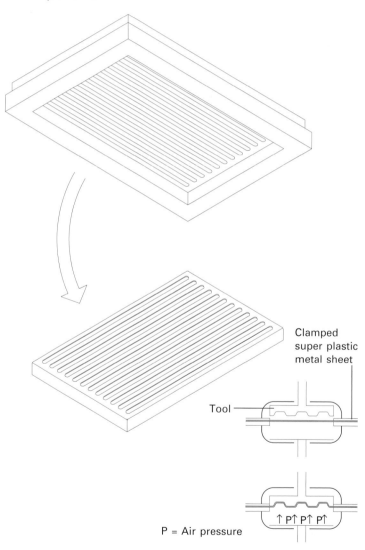

Clamped
super plastic
metal sheet

Tool

Figure 4.22 Cavity forming superplastic aluminium.

P = Air pressure

Drape cavity forming

Here the preheated sheet is placed above the negative tool. Thus the sheet is thickest at the top of the tool surface. The choice, therefore, between conventional cavity forming and drape forming is dependent on where the greater thickness is required in a component.

Bubble forming

As shown in Figure 4.23, in bubble forming the preheated sheet is clamped between a bubble plate and a tool plate. Pressure is applied from below and the superplastic aluminium forms a bubble. The tool is then pressed into this bubble. The air pressure is reversed forcing the sheet or bubble into the detail of the tool. The advantage of this process is that a relatively consistent thickness is achieved. The doubly curved air intakes for the British Aerospace Hawk Training Aircraft, which is flown by the Red Arrows Display Team, are produced by this method.

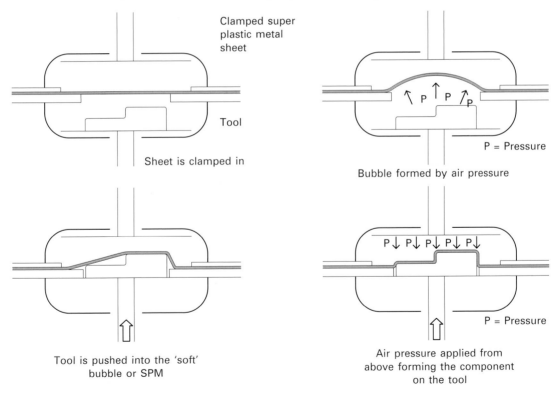

Figure 4.23 Bubble forming superplastic aluminium.

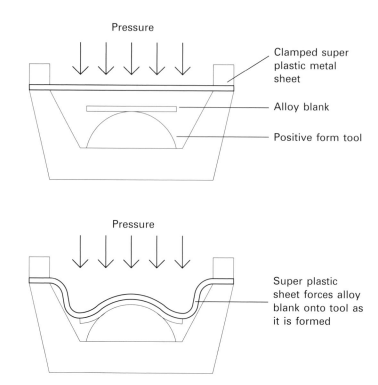

Figure 4.24 Diaphragm forming superplastic aluminium.

Diaphragm forming

This process enables the forming of non-superplastic alloys. This is achieved by clamping a sheet of superplastic aluminium above the sheet to be formed. The diaphragm sheet limits the tendency of the component to buckle. The advantage of this process is that a constant material thickness is achieved. It is a relatively expensive process and has primarily found applications in the production of aerospace and defence components. However, the perforated acoustic ceiling panels in the subway of Stratford Jubilee Line Station, by Wilkinson Eyre Architects, were produced by diaphragm forming.

Back pressure forming

Most alloys develop microporosity, or 'tiny voids', during the superplastic forming process. This is also known as cavitation and it reduces the fatigue characteristics of the alloy. This needs to be avoided in structural applications, such as a Class One or safety critical aircraft component. This can be achieved by forming the component in a chamber at approximately 600 psi (42 kg/cm^2).

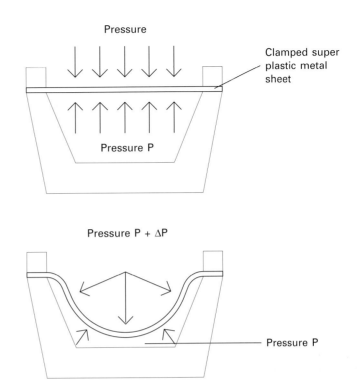

Figure 4.25 Back pressure forming superplastic aluminium.

The pressure is applied to both surfaces of the sheet. Although this process is expensive and is only used for high strength alloys, including 7475 and 8090, it enables parts to be made that are deeper and more intricate. Examples of Class One aerospace components are air intakes or a pressurized cabin door.

The tool used is dependent on the alloy; for Supral alloys with a forming temperature of below 500°C, aluminium tools are used. The tool is produced by either machining a 'block' of aluminium or by sourcing a sand casting. For 5083, 7475 and 8090, which are all formed above 500°C, ferrous tools are required. To ensure that the sheet does not 'weld' itself to the tool, a graphite-based lubricant is used that enables relatively friction-free movement to occur.

It is critical to note that the tool side is the dimensionally most accurate, and the 'air side' should be the exposed or visually significant surface.

Size limitation and design guidance

Overall size is dependent on tooling and available sheet. Taking an architectural example, Superform's maximum size for a formed panel is 3000 × 1800 mm, with

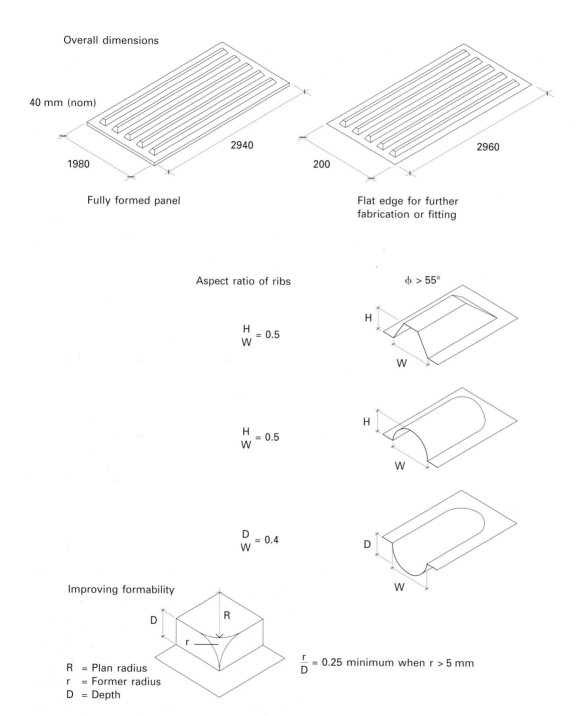

Overall dimensions

40 mm (nom)

2940

1980

Fully formed panel

200

2960

Flat edge for further
fabrication or fitting

Aspect ratio of ribs

$\dfrac{H}{W} = 0.5$

$\phi > 55°$

H

W

$\dfrac{H}{W} = 0.5$

H

W

$\dfrac{D}{W} = 0.4$

D

W

Improving formability

D

R

r

R = Plan radius
r = Former radius
D = Depth

$\dfrac{r}{D} = 0.25$ minimum when r > 5 mm

Figure 4.26 Design guidance for superplastic aluminium components.

a depth of 600 mm. Figure 4.24 gives guidance in radii and aspect ratios for ribbed section; note this is guidance only and particular requirements should be discussed with the forming company. Superplastic aluminium sheet can be combined with other aluminium technologies. It can be more economical to form a panel with a flat edge and clamp it into a pressure plate curtain walling system, as at Gatwick North Piers (architects YRM), or weld an edge to the panel, as at the Financial Times Print Works (architects Nicholas Grimshaw & Partners).

Sainsbury Centre

The Centre for Visual Arts at the University of Norwich, designed by Foster Associates, was originally clad in natural anodized and ribbed superplastic aluminium panels, but they had to be replaced due to premature failure of the superplastic panels. The cause of the failure has never been formally reported. However, it is understood to be the combination of two factors: excessive thinning at the hemispherical corners, and the production of sulphuric acid, caused by water being in contact with the phenolic core leading to corrosion of the aluminium. Too often building 'failures' are buried in insurance settlements. It should be noted that the Sainsbury Centre, which was completed in 1978, was a very innovative application of superplastic aluminium.

The problems encountered illustrate the need to control the specification, physically check the components, and create clear communication with the manufacturer. The physical checking needs to be a statistically significant sample and preferable using a non-destructive test method. The need to check material compatibility is also critical and often this remains the responsibility of the architect or lead designer.

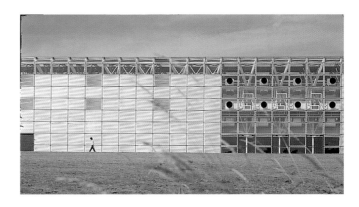

Figure 4.27 Original superplastic aluminium cladding of the Sainsbury Centre, (Architect Foster Associates).

Advantages of superplastic aluminium

Cost savings can be achieved in comparison with fabricated or assembled parts. A single superplastic component will offer weight savings, and structural and visual continuity. When formed in aluminium, the component retains all the advantages of 'conventional' aluminium alloys including the range of finishes and a good strength-to-weight ratio. In comparison to die casting, the tooling costs are significantly lower. Superplastic components have the benefit of offering form and grain to a product or building. Ron Arad's Boop table (see Figure1.9) ably demonstrates the 3D potential of superplastic aluminium.

Figure 4.28 Lords Media Centre by Future System.

Figure 4.29 Welded aluminium semi-monocoque structure of Lords Media Centre fabricated in at the Cornish shipyard, Pendennis of Falmouth.

Further information

BS EN 988   Zinc and zinc alloys. Specification for rolled flat products for building

BS EN 1172   Copper and copper alloys. Sheet and strip for building purposes

BS EN 1173   Copper and copper alloys. Material condition or temper designation

BS EN 1179   Specification for zinc and zinc alloys. Primary zinc

BS EN 10029 Tolerances on dimensions, shape and mass for hot rolled steel plates 3 mm thick or above

BS EN 10088 Stainless steel

BS EN 12588 Lead and lead alloys. Rolled sheets for building purposes

EN 10258   Rolled stainless and heat resistant steel narrow strips and cut length. Tolerances on dimensions and shape

EN 10259   Rolled stainless and heat resistant steel wide strip and sheet/plate. Tolerances on dimensions and shape

References

Alexander, W. and Street, A. (1976). *Metal in the Service of Man,* 6th edn. Penguin Books.

Anderson, J.M. and Gill, J.R. (1988). *Rainscreen Cladding. A guide to design principles and practice.* Butterworths.

Anon (1989). *Superplastic Aluminium Forming.* Welding and Fabrication.

Anon (1993). *Rheinzink Applications in Architecture.* (English edition 1996.)

Baddoo, N., Burgan, R. and Ogden, R. (1997). *Architects' Guide to Stainless Steel.* SCI-P-179 Steel Construction Institute.

Copper Development Association (1985). *Copper in Roofing – Design and Installation.* (Tel. 01707 650711).

Gibb, et al (2000). Cladd:ISS Standardisation of Interfaces in Cladding and Glazing CDROM (CWCT).

Lead Sheet Association (1990). *Lead Sheet Manual, Vols 1–3.*

Witt, C.A. (1997). Zinkberatung e. V. Dusseldorf (1000-2.77). The corrosive behaviour of aluminium in contact with zinc in building construction.

5

Composites

Composite construction can be defined as the bringing together of materials with very different physically properties to form a single component. Combining these materials creates an element of significantly higher performance. Thus the term 'composite' applies equally to: a component manufactured from polymers and stiffened by fibres, such as a carbon fibre yacht mast (see Figure 5.1); a lead clad steel sheet, a cladding panel where the sheet material is bonded to a core (see Figure 5.2); or a flitch beam comprising steel and timber.

Composite construction can divided into two primary forms:

- A micro-composite: the combination of materials to form a rigid and effectively monolithic matrix, such as glass reinforced plastic or carbon fibre resin construction.
- A macro-composite: the bonding or mechanical fixing of dissimilar materials into a layered assembly where the materials remain identifiable in the final component.

Table 5.1 Material properties of carbon fibre

Property	Value
Density	1800 kg/m^3
Young's modulus	325–440 kN/mm^2
Thermal conductivity	*
Co-efficient of thermal expansion	*(Potentially zero)
Corrosion resistance	Excellent
Melting point	*
Recyclability	Poor
Primary embodied energy	*

*Depends on fibre design and orientation
†Data supplied by BRE

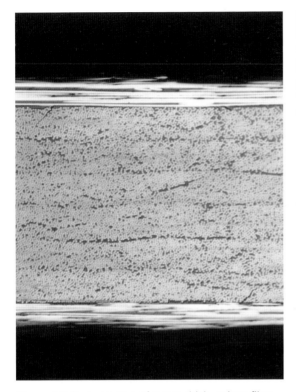

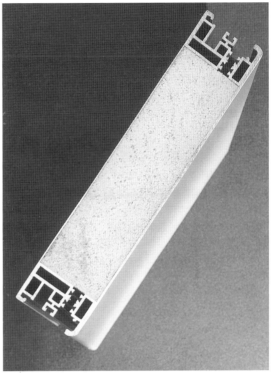

Figure 5.1 Cross-section of 1 mm thick carbon fibre composite, magnified 80 times (courtesy of Professor Paul Smith).

Figure 5.2 Cross-section of a composite metal and extruded polystyrene panel (Aspect 3: courtesy of Corus).

In Figure 5.1, once the 1 mm thick section of carbon fibre has been enlarged by 80 times, it is possible to identify the top and bottom layers of laminate, which are 0.125 mm thick and contain fibres which run across the section. The central layer of the laminate, which is 0.75 mm thick, contains fibre in the orthogonal direction coming out of the plan of the section. The comparison with the cross-section of a composite metal panel (Figure 5.2) clearly shows that the difference between a micro-composite and macro-composite is a question of scale.

Macro-composites

Plywood is a very familiar example of a layered composite. Most grades of plywood are a combination of thin layers of timber bonded together using phenolic glues. Increased strength and consistency of strength is achieved by rotating the direction of the grain in each layer of the ply. The ancient Egyptians are known to have laminated wood, and sheet plywood is in essence an industrialized development of an ancient technique. Early examples of moulded plywood aircraft include the LWF Engineering Company Model V (built in 1919) and the patented monocoque fuselage of the Loughead S-1 (US Patent 1 425 113, 8 August 1922). The latter was produced in a concrete mould and held under pressure for 24 hours by an inflated 'rubber' bag. The S-1 cigar shaped fuselage was a true monocoque without stiffening ribs.

The Second World War brought significant developments in moulded plywood, which included the splint and stretches designed by Charles and Ray Eames. These acted as pre-prototypes for their moulded furniture of the 1950s. One of the most successful aircraft of the Second World War was the de Havaland Mosquito fighter-bomber. This innovative aircraft combined the use of moulded plywood with balsa wood cored macro-composite components, to form a lightweight and rigid monocoque construction. Ordered on 1 March 1940 by the Ministry of Aircraft Production, to a specifi-

Figure 5.3 Mosquito – fighter bomber.

cation developed by de Havaland, the prototype (W40450) made its first flight on 25 November 1940; it was designed and manufactured in less than 11 months! The first Mosquito in operation flew a reconnaissance mission over France on 20 September 1941. The Mosquito proved to be a robust and extremely serviceable aircraft. The balsa wood cores used in the construction of the Mosquito were produced by the Baltek Corporation who are still supplying balsa cores for the construction of boats, planes, and building components. The cargo deck of the Boeing 747 uses a balsa wood cored composite panel.

An advantage of composite construction is that it can be used to combine dissimilar materials. The silicon microelectronic chip is an excellent example of a layered composite on an almost molecular scale, which uses the semiconductive and conductive properties of silicon and aluminium to produce a complex microprocessor. In a composite cladding panel, for example, two metal skins are laminated to an insulating core. This combines the strength and durability of the sheet metal and its finish with the insulating properties of the core material, thus producing a complete building envelope in a single product, combing durability, rigidity and insulation. The relatively thin metal skins, typically 0.5–1.5 mm thick, would not be rigid without the core. It is the spacing of the two sheets that is primarily responsible for the rigidity of the final composite. The wider the spacing the greater the spanning capabilities of the finished product. Also, as the insulation becomes deeper the resistance to thermal transmission increases, proving a lower U-value. Often the limiting factor for structural performance is shearing of the core under load, when tested to the limit. Failure in shear predominately occurs close to the boundary of the core, but not at it.

Le Maison du Peuple at Clichy (by Jean Prouvé, 1939) is an early example of metal cladding that demonstrates the principle of composite construction. The two metal skins are stiffened by the use of a thin board; however, the overall panel stiffness is created by the use of a spring. In many current composite panels the role of the spring is undertaken by an insulating core.

It is possible to categorize metal composite panels by the method of manufacture and core material, which are:

• foamed *in situ* panels
• laminated panels.

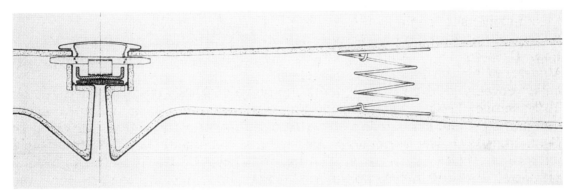

Figure 5.4 Drawing of the panel for Le Maison du Peuple at Clichy by Jean Prouvé, 1939.

Foamed *in situ* panels

The composite action in a foamed *in situ* panel is the result of the foaming of the core material, typically polyurethane, which expands to fill the space between and bonds to the skins of the component. The primary challenge is to achieve consistency in core density and adhesion to the face material without voids. Unfortunately there have been major examples of delamination in poorly controlled horizontally foamed *in situ* composite panels. Between the 1960s and 1980s foamed panel were successfully developed into a reliable technique producing an inexpensive and high performance product that has been extensively used in construction. However, the foaming agent in these panels contained CFCs or HCFCs, which are now implicated in the thinning of the ozone layer.

In the late 1980s and early 1990s carbon dioxide was introduced as an environmentally more responsible foaming agent. This, however, effectively restarted the development cycle for the production of foamed *in situ* panels. Once again variation in core density and delamination occurred. The nature of the foaming agent and method of foaming should be specified by an architect. However, it is difficult to check, and certification of conformity is required unless expensive materials testing is used.

Production methods for foamed *in situ* panels are:

- horizontal foaming
- vertical foaming.

Figure 5.5 Vertical foam panel production mould by Hunter Douglas Construction Elements.

Horizontal foaming

This method of manufacture is readily incorporated in a continuous production process, and only a small minority of horizontally-foamed *in situ* composite panels are now batch produced. Thus panel size is dictated by the production line, with typical standard panel widths of 600, 900 and 1200 mm. Typically the long edges are formed and the short edges are cut which necessitate capping details when the panels are installed. The core materials are predominately polyurethane and polyisocyanurates. The advantage of polyisocyanurates is that they offer a better fire performance. Companies such as Hoesch (Germany), Kingspan (Ireland) and European Profiles (UK) manufacture foamed *in situ* composite panels. Hoesch were responsible for the innovative long span composite structures in the 1960s.

The prototype telephone booth, designed by Klavs Helweg-Larsen, is potentially an excellent example of a foamed *in situ* composite panel product. In 1980 Klavs

Figure 5.6 KTAS telephone booth designed by Klavs Helweg-Larsen.

Helweg-Larsen won a design competition organized by KTAS to design a new telephone box for The Copenhagen Telephone Company. The Klavs Helweg-Larsen design displays line, form rigidity and durability in a product for public use. The structure and form of the booth, consists of two folded stainless steel plates assembled into a box frame by two welded 5 mm-side flanges. The hollow void between the two outer skins was filled with a two-component polyurethane foam, with a density of 60 kg/m^3, thus bonding the two skins together. As Klavs Helweg-Larsen stated 'This ensures a constructive co-operation between the plates so that the structure works as a sandwich construction by absorption of force transversely to the flanges' (Danish Design Council, Casebook 1, 1985; p. 16). However, it is very pertinent to note that when Herning Beholderfabrik put Klavs Helweg–Larsen's design into production with an initial order for 1800 telephone stands, composite construction was dropped. The structure was proving to be too pliable and susceptible to vibrations. The design team also had concerns over the long-term stability of the bond between the polyurethane and the stainless steel; the design life of the stand was 50 years. The structural depth

Figure 5.7 The weld
stainless steel semi-
monocoque of KTAS
telephone booth in
production.

was increased from 60 to 80 mm and a welded semi-monocoque construction all
of stainless steel was adopted, following load testing by the Dantest Laboratory.

Vertical foaming

The primary advantage of vertical-foaming an *in situ* composite panel is that it
minimizes the likelihood of entrapped gases during manufacture. Entrapped
gases can lead, through thermal expansion of entrapped gases, to delamination
of the foam and the panel skin material. Any gases produced as part of the
foaming process should be allowed to escape from the top of the panel during
the production process. Well controlled vertical foaming produces good adhesion
and maintains core density. It is a batch production process; for example, Hunter
Douglas Construction Elements produce vertically-foam panels in heated steel
moulds. This individual and flexible manufacturing technique enables Hunter
Douglas Construction Elements to produce panels of specific sizes to suit the
requirements for each project. This process enables them to manufacture panels

with a maximum length is 12 000 mm; the maximum module width is 1500 mm for both aluminium and steel skin profiles. The blowing agent used is a HCFC with a low ozone depletion factor.

Laminated composite panels

Although currently representing a smaller share of the market, laminated composite panels offer significant advantages over foamed *in situ* production:

- wider range of core materials
- tight control of core density
- variation in size, in width, length and thickness.

Variation in thickness is dependent on the design and cost of edge and interface details. The majority of laminated composites are batch produced to site-specific sizes. The potential core materials include:

- extruded polystyrene
- bead polystyrene
- polyurethane
- polyisocyanurate
- cork or end grain balsa wood
- mineral wool lamella
- foamglas
- aluminium honeycomb
- foamed aluminium.

The choice of core, the material and thickness of the skin and the edge detailing determine the cost and performance capability of a panel. This results is a wide matrix of possibilities which to date remain under-explored. For example, in 1986 the author designed and built a roof for a photographic studio in London, using composite panels spanning 3 m. These were laminated from two skins of 6 mm ply with an extruded polystyrene core (providing a total thickness of 87 mm) and comprised the complete roof build-up to which a PVC roof membrane was bonded.

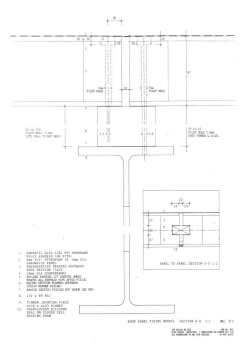

Figure 5.8 Willow Street plywood and extruded polystyrene composite panel (fixing detail).

Once the cores of the panel skins are coated, the assembly is kept under pressure until the initial cure of the adhesive has taken place. This is achieved by using either a platen press or a vacuum press. In a platen press a number of panels or flat components can be laminated at once. A vacuum or bag press is essential for the lamination of shaped components. Here an EPDM sheet is drawn down onto the component by evacuating the air via tiny holes in the steel bed of the press. In both cases the flatness tolerance is dependent on the quality and manufacture of the press. When laminating complex shapes using a vacuum press the method of supporting the component is also critical. Thus the forming of a curved corner panel, for example, is slower and more complex than a flat panel.

Figure 5.9 Vacuum bag press.

One of the limitations of laminated composites is the available width of the core material. It is only comparatively recently that Dow Chemical introduced a 1200 mm wide Styrofoam (extruded polystyrene sheet). Prior to this there was, especially with relatively thin metal skins,

Figure 5.10 Platen press.

a risk of the joints in the core material witnessing through, thus spoiling the flat surface of the finished component. The strength of a laminated assembly is clearly dependent on the bond quality; therefore it is essential that production is closely controlled. It is necessary to control and check the temperature and humidity, and the coating thickness of the adhesive. These procedures should be documented in the manufacturers ISO 9000 quality control procedures. Humidity is critical in the production of composite panels when moisture curing neoprene adhesives are used. Coseley Panel Products, who hot-wire cut Styrofoam to the desired thickness, rib the surface of the core to improve the bond quality. Coseley test the adhesion quality of each batch in house (see Figure 7.11, Chapter 7). It is also important to ensure that the internal surfaces of the panel skins are not contaminated as this can prevent adhesion. To a large extent the production of laminated composites has in the last 20 years moved away from a 'lick and stick' approach to reliable and well-informed industry offering a robust technology.

Expanded polystyrene is cheaper than extruded polystyrene. It is produced by subjecting beads of polystyrene to steam and pressure. However, its thermal performance is not as effective as extruded polystyrene. It also shrinks with age. This predominantly occurs in the first 2 weeks after manufacture. Thus expanded polystyrene should be aged prior to manufacture into a laminated composite.

In designing a composite panel it is essential that a balanced composite is produced, otherwise the panel will act like a bi-metallic strip and will bend. Thermal bowing is inevitable with composite panels; the outer skin will be warmed by the sun and darker colours can easily reach 80°C. Thus the external skin will expand causing the panel to bow outwards. If the panel colour is too dark or the front skin is over-restrained, delamination will result. It is also critical to remain within the stable operating temperature of the core material. If flatness at all times is an essential technical or visual criteria, a rainscreen panel should be specified as the rainscreen panel itself is free to expand in a linear manner and is subject to less of a thermal gradient. In designing the junctions of composite assemblies, negative thermal movement can also prove critical and should be thoroughly checked.

Extruded polystyrene, such as Styrofoam, is currently produced using a HCFC foaming agent 142B, which has an ozone depletion factor of 0.06 (where 1 is the ODF of a CFC). Dow Chemical has introduced three grades of Styrofoam, which are produced using a CO_2 foaming agent, which has an ODF of zero. However, there is a reduction in thermal resistance so a thicker board is required for the same U-value. To date, Dow Chemical has not produced a grade of CFC-free board suitable for forming composite panels. Insulated composite panels can provide a very low U-value and thus once installed contribute significantly to the reduction of CO_2 production.

Fire Performance

In some applications fire performance is of critical importance and with some building types this has been prompted by The Loss Prevention Council. In many building types it is not necessary to specify a totally non-combustible assembly. Many metal skinned composite panel systems have Class O to BS 476 faces and a flammable core. Therefore they will not burn easily, despite having a high percentage of construction, within the cross-section that is flammable. Concern about fire performance and the need to build on or near boundaries, for example, has lead to the development of mineral wool lamella-cored panels. Using steel skins and a mineral wool lamella core it is possible to produce panels with a full 1 hour fire rating, offering integrity and insulation. Mineral wool lamella is formed by bonding the mineral wool fibres into a panel with the fibres at 90° to the panel surface. However, the panels are significantly heavier and offer less thermal resistance than extruded polystyrene of the same thickness.

Micro-composites

There is now a wide range of materials that can be used to form micro-composites and there is a growing acceptance of this technology. Basically, a selected fibre is held in a resin matrix, which is typically set by the application of pressure and heat. The mechanical properties of the component can be varied by the type of fibre selected, the resin, and the orientation of the fibres. The fibres are usually used in continuos filaments or as woven or sown fabrics. Specific inserts can also be introduced to create areas of selected stiffness; for example, the nose cone of a formula one racing car has an aluminium insert within the layers of carbon fibre composite, which is designed to crumple in the event of a front end crash.

The principle fibres used in a micro-composite are:

• glass
• carbon
• aramid including Kevlar
• boron
• harvested fibres – flax and jute.

Micro-composites offer the architect, engineer or designer almost infinite control of the resultant component. This offers a design freedom that can produce components of optimum performance. The fibre type can be varied depending on the required stiffness, the resin, and the orientation of the fibres and their density. With the ability to weave the fibre, a direct use of textile technology, it is possible to control the performance characteristic in both directions and thus achieve a highly

Figure 5.11 Computer model of a Formula One racing car carbon fibre safety monocoque chassis, courtesy of Advanced Composites.

efficient structure. Unlike an extrusion, the overall thickness of the material can be varied at particular load points and inserts introduced.

Fibre selection

The primary characteristic of each type of fibre is:

• glass: low cost yet relatively low strength
• carbon fibre: higher in cost offering excellent stiffness

- aramid including Kevlar: a very tough fibre offering excellent resistance to extension and good energy absorbing properties
- boron: extremely stiff lightweight fibre, also expensive. Boron fibres are used to form the spine of the B52 bomber.

The range of resins used includes; epoxy, phenolics, and polyesters. The primary advantage of polyester is that it is cheaper. However, it offers lower performance and is also problematic in application with concerns of health and safety and the environment. Phenolics offer the benefit of enhanced performance in fire with low toxicity in the products of combustion. Thus phenolics are often used to form the linings of aircraft and trains. The disadvantage of phenolics is that they are relatively brittle. The fire performance of an epoxy resin can be enhanced by the addition of fire retardants, creating a balance between mechanical and fire performance.

The advantages of micro-composites are:

- lightweight components with a high strength-to-weight ratio
- components that are very strong and stiff
- ablity to orientate fibres with the direction of principle stress and thus achieve high structural efficiency
- excellent corrosion resistance
- high resistance to impact damage (dependant on fibre selection)
- effectively zero thermal expansion, if required
- excellent fatigue characteristics
- mouldablity: complex shapes can be readily made
- affordable one-off, prototype, or short production runs
- press moulding and resin transfer moulding are medium to high volume processes.

Production methods

The production process for micro-composites requires heat to activate the curing mechanism. This also reduces the viscosity of the resin, assisting it to flow, and the application of pressure to compact and consolidate the laminate.

The primary methods of manufacture are:

- contact moulding (or hand lay-up)
- vacuum bag moulding
- autoclave moulding
- press moulding

- resin transfer moulding
- filament winding
- pultrusion

Contact moulding

In essence this is a very simple process; the reinforcing material is laid into a mould and the resin is applied by brush or roller. Successive layers are built up as required, with each layer being consolidated to minimize air entrapment by rollering. Dr Les Norword of resin suppliers, Scott Barder, states that 'fibre reinforced plastic is one of the few materials where the moulder/fabricator both manufactures the component and material simultaneously'. The exception to this is prepeg, which is a method of pre-engineering the material prior to fabrication. Moulds are typically made of timber or fibre-reinforced plastic (FRP), and prior to the application of the reinforcing material the mould is waxed and a release agent applied [**3]. At this stage a gel coat is often applied; gel coats are thixotropic resins which will adhere to near vertical surfaces. The surface in contact with the mould is a high quality visual surface and can incorporate texture from the mould tool.

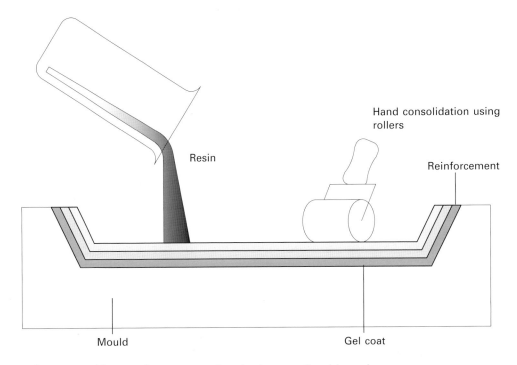

Figure 5.12 Contact moulding a polymer composite, also know as 'hand lay-up'.

There is effectively no limit to the size of component that can be produced. Often the governing factor is the maximum size for transportation. Capital investment is small, and has found widespread applications, including boat building and architectural components such as cladding panels. However, the process is dependent on the skill of the applicator, and control of the thickness can be difficult. Mould fabrication is also a highly skill process. Contact moulding is relatively slow; for example, a component such as a cladding panel would be produced on the basis of one panel per mould per day. Therefore, to meet a project programme more than one mould is used even if the project is fully modular or completely standardized. The resins are typically air cured at ambient temperature, which can result in entrapment of volatiles produced from the curing process.

Health and Safety legislation, restricting exposure to emission of volatile organic components, is resulting in a decline in the use of contact moulding. It is also a relatively slow and labour intensive process. An option is the spray application of the resin and fibre reinforcement. Contact moulding is not appropriate for components that require high structural integrity.

As with all moulded products it is essential to design the component so that it will be released from the former. A minimum mould angle of 1° is typical. However, 90° sides can be produced. A FRP lay-up will shrink as it cures by 0.1–0.4%, which needs to be allowed for in the mould design but aids release.

Vacuum bag moulding

A vacuum is formed under a sealed bag applying an even pressure to the prepreg lay-up in the mould. The pressure is up to 1 atmosphere, 14 psi (1 kg/cm^2), and the assembly is then heated in an oven to between 60 and 180°C depending on the resin selected. The high quality visual surface is against the mould whereas the bag side is less precise. Unlike metal-faced composite panels, and for small to medium sized components, the bag is actually a moulded sheet of silicone, which itself can be formed for a specific component. The vacuum bag moulding method is appropriate for components of complex forms with double curvature and can be used for large components. The mould costs are low; however, for the highest structural integrity higher pressures are required.

Autoclave moulding

This can be defined as the application of heat and pressure. As in the vacuum bag method the prepreg lay-up is subjected to an even pressure from a vacuum formed within a sealed bag. However, an additional pressure of up to 100 psi

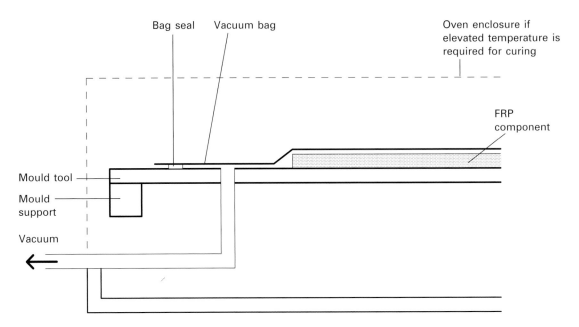

Figure 5.13 Vacuum bag moulding a polymer composite.

(70 kg/cm^2) is applied in a heated pressure vessel. Typically the temperature of the autoclave is 180°C, but this is dependent on the chosen resin. This produces laminates with a minimum void content and the control of laminate thickness is much greater than in the vacuum bag method. The pressure is maintained throughout the total heating and cooling process. The monocoque safety cage and chassis of Formula One racing cars are autoclaved. Primary structure aircraft components, such as wings spars, are also manufactured by this method.

Press moulding

This is a compression moulding process. The tools are typically cast or machined metal and are in male and female matched halves. The pressure is usually applied hydraulically and heating is typically provided by oil, steam or electrically. If steam or oil is used passages are built into the tool. The prepreg is usually performed on a separate former or charge to facilitate rapid handing.

This method produces components of very high accuracy and high quality. The tooling is expensive and can be automated; this method is therefore suited to high volume production runs.

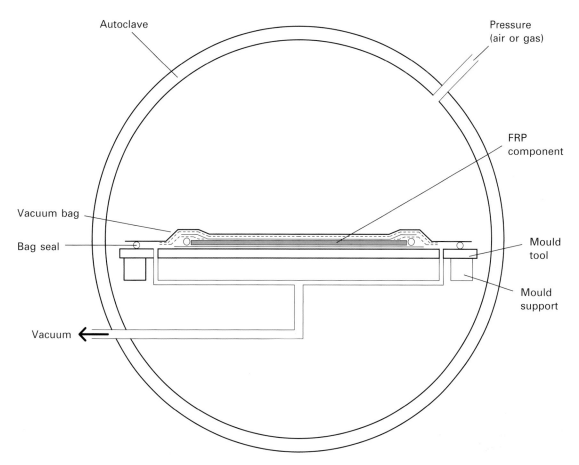

Figure 5.14 Autoclave moulding a polymer composite.

Resin transfer moulding

Dry performed reinforcement, and core material when required, is placed in the lower half of a match tool. The tools are closed and clamped, and catalysed resin is injected under pressure. As the matched tool is subject to only 2–3 bar, tools can be made of FRP, metal lined FRP, and aluminium. Typically resin transfer moulding (RTM) is cost effective for the production of over 100 components, and for components up to 6000 mm long. Components of close tolerance, which do not need machining, are produced with a good cycle time; for example, a 5 m component can be produced in 25 min including gel coat stage. RTM has the advantage of being closed during the consolidation and curing process; thus emission of volatile organic compounds is minimized.

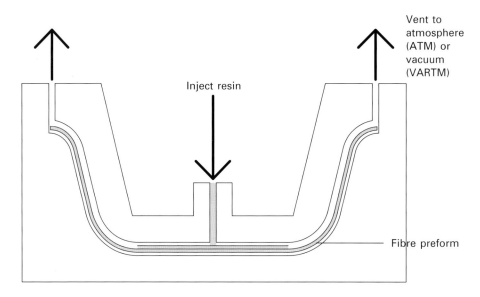

Figure 5.15 Resin transfer moulding (RTM) a polymer composite.

Vacuum assisted resin injection, or VARI, is in essence a variant of resin transfer moulding where a partial vacuum is applied to consolidate the reinforcement and remove air.

Filament winding

Continuous fibres or tape are wound onto a rotating mandrel. It is critical to control the angle of feed of the fibres to the rotating mandrel. Resin is accurately applied via a resin bath or drip fed. The consolidation pressure is achieved through the tensioning of the fibres as they are wound onto the mandrel. Power transmission shafts, landing gear struts, and pressure vessels are manufactured by this process. A limitation of filament winding is that the visually high quality surface is the internal surface, which is in contact with the mandrel.

Pultrusion

The pultrusion process is described in Chapter 2 (see pp. 53–59).

Sandwich construction

Micro-composites can form the skins of a macro-composite panel or sandwich panel. There are two main manufacturing methods: single-stage cure, and two-stage cure. In single stage the lay-up is carried out on a single tool. The prepreg is applied to the tool surface, followed by a layer of adhesive if required. The core is then positioned and if necessary, coated with a second layer of adhesive; the closing prepreg is then applied. The complete assembly is vacuum bagged and heated or autoclaved if required. In two-stage curing the skins are manufactured by the vacuum bag method or autoclaving and bonded to the core again in an oven or autoclave. The process is essentially similar to the production of metal composite panels except for the application of heat and greater pressure when necessary.

Pre-impregnated sheet

The dilemma of how to deliver fibre and resin in a precise and controlled quantity has led to the development of pre-impregnated sheets of resin-coated fibre or fabric. Pre-impregnated sheet, know as prepreg, is a roll of resin-coated orientated fibre supported and separated by paper to facilitate its use. The process is outstandingly simple, although some of the chemistry is extremely sophisticated. The fabric is loaded on to the prepreg line, as is a roll of release paper. The paper is then coated with resin, rather like ink in a printing press. The fibres are introduced and, depending on the thickness, a second release paper is applied to the top. The prepreg sheet is then heated to induce an initial set. The rolls of prepreg sheet are then refrigerated to extend their shelf time.

Each batch is subjected to strict quality control. Advanced Composite Materials of Derbyshire and Ohio carry out the following minimum checks: weight of resin, and fibre density on 300 mm squares sampled from each batch. Prepreg are easier to handle and result in a lower void content than wet laid methods. Essentially it is a 'filo pastry'-like material of precise and known mechanical properties.

Figure 5.16 Prepreg line at Advanced Composites.

Low temperature resins

The past 15 years has seen the development of resins that can be cured at relatively low temperatures. This has greatly reduced the capital and running

Figure 5.17 Prototype composite modular train station canopy.

costs of the production of micro- composites. This has advantages to the aircraft industry in reducing lead time and development costs. It has also released the potential for the use of carbon fibre more extensively in the construction industry. Large components can either be factory produced, say 27 metres long, or

Figure 5.18 Detail of the prototype composite modular train station canopy.

laid up on site, if too large to transport, size is not limited by the process. The increase in temperature required to cure the prepreg is created by warm air (65°C) in a temporary tent.

Brookes Stacey Randall with Advanced Composites and Taywood Engineering have conducted research for DETR into the application of micro-composites in the construction industry. Part of this research has been the production of a modular canopy for Railtrack to be used on smaller or parkway stations. This is composite of carbon fibre with a Styrofoam core. The gull wing section has a carbon fibre spine beam necessary to achieve the 10 m span. This one-piece component measures 10.9 × 4.2 m and weighs 1200 kg. Details are totally integrated, from the drainage gully to the mounting for up-lighters and signage.

Design freedom

It is not possible to ask a composite component 'what it wants to be' as Louis Kahn might have done; there are perhaps too many variables and only the beginnings of an established approach. However, this should encourage exploration of this material, particularly as the cost factors continue to fall.

Further information

BS 2782	Methods of testing plastics (for example BS 2782-721A Determination of resin flow from resin impregnated glass fabric)
BS 3496 (1989)	Specification for E glass fibre chopped strand mat for reinforcement of polyester and other liquid laminating systems
BS 4549 Part 1 (1997)	Guide to the preparation of a scheme to control the quality of glass reinforced polyester mouldings.
BS 5350 Part C6 (1997)	Determination of bond strength in direct tension in sandwich panels
BS EN 314	Plywood. Bond quality
BS EN 315	Plywood. Dimensional tolerances
BS EN 635	Plywood. Classification of surface appearance
BS EN 636	Plywood. Specifications
BS EN 1072 (1995)	Plywood. Structural and bending properties

BS EN 2375	Resin pre-impregnated materials, production batch sampling
BS EN 2557 (1997)	Carbon fibre pre-impregnates. Determination of mass per unit area
BS EN 2558 (1997)	Carbon fibre pre-impregnates. Determination of volatile content
BS EN 2559 (1997)	Carbon fibre pre-impregnates. Determination of the resin and fibre content and the mass of fibre per unit area
BS EN 2560 (1998)	Carbon fibre pre-impregnates. Determination of the resin flow
BS EN 2561 (1995)	Carbon fibre plastics. Unidirectional laminates. Tensile test parallel to the fibre direction
BS EN 2562 (1997)	Carbon fibre plastics. Unidirectional laminates. Flexural test parallel to the fibre direction
BS EN 2563 (1997)	Carbon fibre plastics. Unidirectional laminates. Determination of the apparent inter-laminar shear strength
BS ISO 1172(1996)	Textile-glass reinforced plastics, test methods
BS EN ISO 10352 (1997)	Plastics, fibre-reinforced, mass per unit area determination
BS EN ISO 12114 (1997)	Fibre reinforced, cure characteristics determination

References

Anon. (1985). DD Casebook 1 KTAS i Gadebilledet Street Signal KTAS. Danish Design Council.

Beukers, A. and Hinte, E. (1999). *Lightness – The inevitable renaissance of minimum energy structures*. 010 Publishers, Rotterdam

Brookes, A.J. (1998*). Cladding of Buildings*, 3rd edn. E&FN Spon.

Brookes, A.J., Fursdon, A., Randall, N. and Stacey, M. (1992). *Aspect 2 Launch Catalogue*. ABA

Halliwell, S.M. (1999). Architectural use of polymer composites. BRE Digest 442.

Halliwell, S.M. (1999). Advanced polymer composites in construction. BRE IP7/99.

Hollaway, L. ed (1990). *Polymers and Polymer Composites in Construction*. Thomas Telford.

Shahidi, E. (1987). Introduction to Advanced Composites. Advance Composite Group.

6

Glass as a component

'Glass is very strong but fragile. To be fragile means that is breaks easily, particularly under shock or sharp loading. All this we know. Glass is after all a material with which we are all familiar' (Peter Rice, 1994).

It is the duality of glass that is so often referred to: its strength and fragility; its transparency and presence. Usually flat, it is fully castable. Apparently solid it is like a 'supercooled' fluid. Inert yet it will leak salts into ponding water. It is almost a schizophrenic material, which is the 'Helen of Troy' of the Modern Movement. Mistakenly thought of, in my opinion, by some as a non-material, it is a void in their architecture. It is regarded as self-cleaning when is should be regularly maintained. Glass is a positive environmental filter and structural component. It can provide colour, surface translucency, and can transform from day and night. It is frustrating when used unwisely yet provides delight in the hands of an informed architect or engineer.

This ancient material is now used with increasing confidence, particularly in the last 25 years. This is a result of considerable testing by manufacturers, such as

Table 6.1 Material properties of glass

Property	Value
Density	2793 kg/m^3
Young's modulus	70.3 KN/mm^2
Thermal conductivity	1–1.5 W/mK
Co-efficient of thermal expansion	8.5×10^{-6}–9.5×10^{-6} per K
Corrosion resistance	Excellent
Melting point	1500°C
Recyclability	Excellent
Primary embodied energy[*]	41 GJ/m^3

[*]Data supplied by BRE.

Pilkington, and research, testing and development carried out by architects and engineers on specific projects. For example, Peter Rice at 'Les Serres' Parc de la Villete, or the research undertaken by the Dutch engineer, Robert Nissje, who worked on the Sonsbeck Pavilion. He discovered when load testing glass rods as potential structural columns that 'each glass rod made a noise like dolphins singing just before it shattered'.[1]

Glass is perhaps the first building element to be self evidently a component. The window pane, due to the stark material difference between the frame, the wall and the pane, identifies and isolates the glass as a finite element, fabricated off site and cut to a predetermined size. Glass, once toughened or fabricated into a double glazed unit, becomes a predetermined component; its

Figure 6.1 Boat Pavilion Streatley (architect Brookes Stacey Randall).

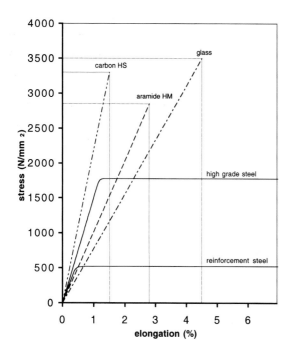

Figure 6.2 Comparative structural performance of glass, steel and timber.

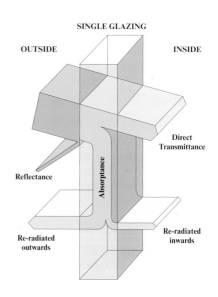

Figure 6.3 Solar radiant heat diagram for single glazing.

[1]Robert Nissje, Lecture at Architectural Association, London, 1993.

size cannot be altered, quality is totally predicable, as are the performance criteria.

Chemistry of glass

Glass is a solid with an amorphous or random non-crystalline structure. It has a similar structure to a liquid, however some consider the description of glass as a 'supercooled' fluid a misnomer as it cannot flow. Great care in formulation and the cooling process are required to ensure that it remains non-crystalline in structure. The most common form of glass is soda lime glass which is formed from three primary compounds: silica, which comprises silicone and oxygen (SiO_2); soda or sodium carbonate (Na_2CO_3); and lime or calcium oxide (CaO). Intense heat must be added to these to make glass. Silica will fuse to make glass at 1726°C; the addition of soda and lime reduces the melting point to 1600°C, offering considerable economy in production.

Examined on a molecular level the silicone and oxygen form a network of bonds, with randomly scattered calcium and sodium atoms. It is because of this random structure that glass has almost no ductility and is subject to brittle failure. This is also the reason for the transparency of glass. The presence of trace elements and compounds modifies the colour of a glass. Common soda lime glass typically contains 0.1% iron oxide, usually an impurity in the sand, which causes the characteristic green colour. Body tinted glasses can be produced by the addition of specific compounds; for example, cobalt oxide produces blue glass, or selenium pink.

Why glass breaks

There are two primary reasons why annealed glass will break easily: first, the presence of calcium and sodium and the relatively weak atomic bonds; and second, the presence of surface imperfections. These are known as Griffith Flaws in honour of A. A. Griffith who in 1921 suggested that it was invisible surface imperfections that explain the difference between the theoretical strength of glass of 20 000 N/mm^2 and the test results of a freshly drawn glass fibre of 5000 N/mm^2. Button and Pye (1993) suggested that 'the presence of Griffith flaws appears to be attributable to contamination of the surface by particles of dust and moisture vapour'. The suggested mechanism is that stress concentrated by a flaw disrupts the weaker inter-atomic bonds and failure occurs.

This quality is positively used in cutting annealed glass, the cutter effectively uniting a series of flaws. The avoidance of scratches and/or shelling in installed glass is critical for its long-term durability. Annealed glass breaks into large irregularly shaped shards, which can prove dangerous. This pattern can be seen in Marcel Duchamp's painting 'Bride Stripped Bare by Her Own Bachelors, Even' which was painted on glass between 1915 and 1923 and unfortunately dropped by its owner, Katherine Dreier, in 1926. The cracks have since become an integral part of this painting.

Discovery of glass

Glass was probably first discovered in the form of naturally occurring examples of fused silica. This takes two forms: when lightening strikes the heat generated can fuse the sand into long, thin tubules, called fulgurites, or petrified lightening. The second form

Figure 6.4 'Bride Stripped Bare by Her Own Bachelors, Even', The Large Glass, 1915–23 by Marcel Duchamp.

is caused by the intense heat of a volcanic eruption that can sometimes fuse rock and sand, which if cooled rapidly forms into a glass, called obsidian. This has the same chemical composition as granite, but forms glass due to the rapid cooling or quenching which prevents the formation of a crystalline structure, clearly apparent in granite. American Indians used obsidian to form knives and arrowheads. Pliny credits Phoenician merchants with the discovery of glass in 4000 BC, as an accidental consequence of making a fire on a sandy beach.

This chapter provides a brief summary of the development of glass from the age of enlightenment to the present, and will focus on glass processes that are still available. For further information on the development of glass making techniques, see Button and Pye (1993) and Wigginton (1996).

Brief chronology of the development of glass production

1680s–1830s	Spun glass or crown process: maximum size by mid nineteenth century was 1676 mm in diameter, typical pane size was 559 × 368 mm. Small yet optically brilliant glass. The last major crown producer ceased production in 1872.
1687	In France Perrot develops cast polished glass.
1773	British Cast Plate Manufactures founded at Ravenshead: maximum size 3600 × 1800 mm.
1830s	Improved cylinder process. Maximum size approximately 1.5 m², panes were typically rectangular.
1838	J.T. Chance invents 'Patent Plate', a polishing technique for blown cylinder glass.
1851	Crystal Palace glazed with 'Patent Plate' 254 × 1250 mm, and a sheet of polished plate 5800 × 3000 mm exhibited.
1896	Mechanized cylinder process developed by John Lubber. Introduced to Britain in 1910 by Pilkington; glass up to approximately 9000 × 1800 mm possible.
1903	Laminated glass discovered by Edouard Benedictus.
1904	Belgian glassmaker Fourcault's first patent for drawn glass manufacture. Width between 1900 and 2300 mm possible.
1905	Colburn drawn process patented in USA; maximum width also 2300 mm.
1920s	Ground and polished plate perfected, including: Bicheroux rolled plate process and Ford Motor Company mechanized plate production.
1928	Securit vertically toughened glass invented.
1938	Pilkington introduce continuous production, including automatic twin grinding and polishing of both surfaces.
1952–59	Float Process invented and introduced by Pilkington at St Helens.

Float process

The float process is an example of a manufacturing technique invented in Britain, realized in this country and is now used throughout the world. It was invented by Pilkington in St Helens in 1952. By 1955 a full-scale production unit was producing glass 2.5 m wide. However, the float process was not introduced for commercial production until 1959 after 'it made 100,000 tonnes of waste glass

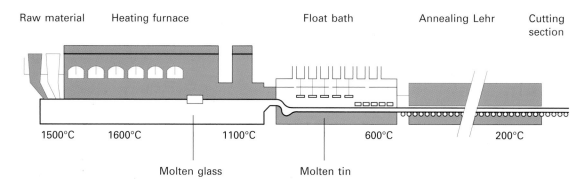

Figure 6.5 Diagram of the float process.

before it sold its first square metre of float [glass]' (Rawson, 1996). Part of this timeframe was used to prudently patent the process. The main stages of the float process are: melting of the raw material and cullet (recycled glass) in a furnace at 1500–1600°C; the molten glass then flows onto the bath of tin at 1100°C; the glass leaves the float tank at about 600°C and into the annealing lehr where it is cooled to 100°C; it is then checked and cut to size. It is essential that the complete float process remains continuous.

Figure 6.6 End wall of the Sainsbury Centre Norwich, architect Foster Associates.

Although the investment is high, estimated as £80 000 000 in 1996, the product is a high volume, economical and yet high quality glass. As the process is continuous the change from clear glass to a body tinted glass takes 4 days. The molten glass floats on the tin because of the higher density of tin. The glass on the bed of molten tin is normally 6–7 mm thick; thinner sheet is produced by stretching the glass and thicker glass by controlled damming. The typical range of thickness is from 3 to 25 mm. Pilkington can produce float glass to 0.5 mm thickness. Their current maximum sheet width is 3500 mm, although 3210 mm is the standard production width for European float glass. The standard maximum length for float glass is 6000 mm; this is a result of the mechanical handling equipment that stocks the glass after cutting. Many float lines will produce sheets of 10 or 12 m in length, if ordered specially. The mechanical handing of a sheet potentially 12×3.2 m requires particular consideration. As the float process produces a continuous ribbon of glass, the operative constraints are primarily weight, handling and transportation. The annealed glass end walls of the Sainsbury Centre, Norwich, by Foster Associates are 7500×2500 mm wide and 15 mm thick. They were produced by Saint-Roch of Belgium and edge-finished by Solaglas.

Safety Glass

There are three potential types of safety glass:

- toughened glass
- laminated glass
- annealed glass.

Figure 6.7 Montmartre Funicular Canopy (architect François Deslaugiers, engineers Marc Malinowsky of Groupe ALTO).

Annealed glass may appear surprising as a safety glass since in thin sheet form it is relatively easily broken. However, 15 mm annealed glass is recognized as a safety glass by part N of the English and Welsh Building Regulations. It should be remembered that unless detailed with great care, as in Montmartre funicular (see Figure 6.7) canopy engineered by Groupe ALTO, it is not possible to use bolted details with annealed glass, due to the high stress at the fixing.

Toughened glass

The process of heating glass to 525–650°C and then rapidly cooling or quenching, causes the outer surfaces to contract more rapidly than the centre. Thus the surface of the glass goes into compression and the core into tension; this effectively pre-stresses the glass. Toughened glass can sustain four to five times the stress of annealed glass. It is therefore capable of withstanding greater bending forces, for example under wind load, and accepting the relatively high loads and stress of a bolted fixing. Yet is vital to remember in the design of glass assemblies, particularly for public buildings, that the Young's Modulus of the glass is unchanged and it is no stiffer than annealed. Therefore, the design of a toughened glass assembly is often governed by acceptable visual deflection criteria and not the stress capacity of the glass.

Once toughened, glass cannot be cut or drilled. Further processing is possible, such as etching or polishing, as long as this does not penetrate the zone of surface compression. If struck by a hard and sharp impact of sufficient force, toughened glass breaks suddenly with the release of the entrapped stress. Toughened glass breaks into relatively harmless nodules. The speed with which toughened glass breaks is used to make very high speed shutters for specialist cameras.

Figure 6.8 The 'safe' nodules of toughened glass when shattered.

When using thermally toughened glass it is not possible to create sharp pointed triangles of toughened glass as the tips will 'melt off' as the sheet is heated to 650°C. Typically for long units, such as beams, an aspect ratio of 10 to 1 needs to be maintained. Toughened glass is a Class A safety glass as defined by BS 6262.

It is also possible to chemically toughen glass and this is often used to toughen glass below 3 mm thick, which proves to be problematic in the thermal toughening process.

Development of Toughened Glass

Prince Rupert (1619–1682), nephew of Charles 1 of England and Commander of the Royalist cavalry and eventually his Commander in Chief in the English Civil War, is credited with the discovery of toughened glass in the form of a droplet of glass quenched in cold water. These toughened glass droplets were little more than a curiosity in the court. The droplet would resist being struck by a hammer yet would shatter into characteristic small pieces if the tail was snapped off. Michael Wigginton (1996) in his book *Glass in Architecture* suggests that the phenomenon was known since the Middle Ages.

Although experimental toughening of glass was known in the nineteenth century, it was not until 1928 that the Compagnies Réunies des Glaces et Verres Spéciaux du Nord de la France produced a reliable toughening process and gave it the product name 'Securit'. They suspended a sheet of annealed glass vertically in an electrical furnace and then rapidly cooled it with blown cold air on both surfaces. The disadvantage of this process is the row of tong marks along the top edge of the glass sheet. By the early 1930s Pilkington had introduced its own vertically-toughened glass under the trade name Armourplate. They advertized its strength theatrically by loading the glass with three baby elephants and their two keepers.[2] Armourplate was used on the Daily Express building designed by Owen Williams with Ellis, Clarke & Gallannaugh and completed in 1932.

Although it is still possible to specify vertically-toughened glass, the horizontal or roller hearth method now predominates as it avoids the tong marks, stretching and distortion. The glass is heated in a roller hearth

[2]Dinah Stobbs, a Pilkington Archivist, reported in private correspondence with the author that, 'the original insurance policies taken out to cover any risk to the elephants when hired for a one day photo session [stated]. The sum insured was £110 per elephant and the risk was taken by 21 intrepid Lloyds underwriters – O, they of little faith' The insurance proved unnecessary.

Figure 6.9 Pilkington demonstrate the strength of toughened glass by loading a sheet with three baby elephants and their two keepers.

141

and then both surfaces are quenched with blown air. Although the horizontal method produces glass of higher optical quality than the vertical method, it is not as flat as float glass since horizontally-toughened glass exhibits roller wave distortion as a direct result of the process. The limits of acceptable roller wave distortion should be set in the specification and if flatness is a critical criterion for the project and a safety glass is required, then a laminated glass should be used.

It is possible for toughened glass to fail apparently spontaneously due to nickel sulphide inclusions. Nickel sulphide impurities within the glass 'seed' and expand causing the glass to shatter. The problem of inclusions can be overcome primarily by careful management of the furnace avoiding sulphide as a by-product of fuel combustion and by heat-soaking after quenching. Heat soaking is essentially a destructive quality control process. If a sheet of toughened glass has an inclusion it will shatter it there and then. It is rejected safely in the glass works and not on site or in the building's life. Pilkingtons quote a reliability of 99% for the heat-soaking process. The only current European Standard for heat soaking is DIN 18516 Part 4. This sets out the heat-soaking test as 8 hours in an oven at $290 \pm 5°C$. A CEN standard for heat soaking of toughened glass is under consideration, but as yet a draft standard has not been produced.

Many reported spontaneous failures of toughened glass, which have deeply perturbed building owners, could have had other causes rather than inclusions. These include edge damage during installation; glass to metal contact due to poor details or incorrect installation; 'forcing' the glass into position due to poor control of tolerance, which is a particular problem in framed curved glass. These last two are often triggered by thermal expansion. Vandalism can also be a problem, particularly the shooting out of panes of toughened glass for the 'thrill' of seeing it shatter!

Heat strengthened glass

This produced by a similar process to toughened glass. The sheets are heated to 650–700°C, however it is cooled more gently producing less compressive stress in the surface of the glass. Heat strengthened glass is not a safety glass and breaks into shards just like annealed glass. The primary advantage of heat strengthened glass is an increased tolerance of stress induced by thermal movement and it is often used with coatings, which may result in a higher thermal range in the installed glass or double glazed unit.

Laminated glass

Edouard Benedictus whilst experimenting with cellulose nitrate in 1903, accidentally knocked over a flask containing the solidified liquid. To his surprise the glass broke yet adhered to the cellulose nitrate. He realized the potential for impact resistant glazing, however initial formulations proved not to be stable in sunlight and discoloured. By 1927 the Ford Motor Company had introduced a windscreen laminated with cellulose. In the 1930s DuPont, working in a consortium of American manufacturers, developed polyvinyl butyl laminate (PVB) and it was first used in car windscreens in 1938.

When laminating two or more sheets, the glass is washed to remove any contaminants and an interlayer is laid between the glass sheet. This layered assembly is heated to softening point, which also expels any trapped air. A roller then compresses it and the edges are sealed. The sheet then enters an autoclave under pressures of 12–14 kg/m^2 at 135–145°C. It is the application of pressure and heat that distinguishes an autoclave from an oven or a furnace. The PVB interlayer becomes clear when laminated under pressure.

The edge of a laminated sheet can only be left exposed externally if a clear edge tape is used; an exposed edge of PVB alone is likely to fog. Similarly, laminated glazing should not be 'stood' in water in an unsealed glazing channel, emphasizing the need for effective drainage to be designed into a transom section.

PVB remains the predominant interlayer with which to produce laminated glass. If toughened glass is used in a laminated assembly a cast resin is often used, such as a cold curing acrylic, due to its greater tolerance of roller wave distortion from the toughening process. When using a cold curing acrylic resin the development of air bubbles needs to be controlled, as they can be unsightly.

Drawn glass

Drawn glass is still produced in Poland, Russia and USA. The process involves drawing the syrupy molten glass up a tower approximately 100 feet tall. An annealed glass of acceptable visual quality is produced, although it is not free from distortion. Drawn glass was effectively superseded by the float glass process, which produces glass of a constant thickness and superb optical quality. Drawn glass has two advantages: economy, and relative ease of changing the chemistry of the melt and thus the colour of the glass produced. In Poland and Russia production of drawn glass is a result of low capital investment cost and produces an economical glass, which is primarily used in horticultural greenhouses, both domestic and commercial. In North America, drawn glass is used to produce glasses of a particular colour, such as blue or 'water white glass', as the process although continuous is more readily changed than the float process.

Studio glass

Just as Pilkington were launching float glass onto the market and licensing it to others, in the early 1960s small scale kilns were developed to enable studio glass to be produced. Similar to studio pottery kilns, they are capable of producing the 1500–1600°C to melt glass. This antithesis of the continuous float process facilitated a craft based exploration of the quality of glass. As stated by Tony Ford, Director of the Crafts Council when reviewing the submissions for the Jerwood Prize for

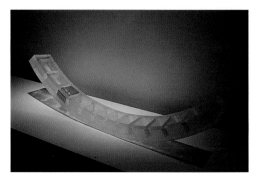

Figure 6.10 Sequence1 (1997) by Galia Amsel: cast and slumped glass polished with sandblasted texture with silver and copper leaf.

Applied Art 1998: Glass, 'The advances in technique and in aesthetic, as well as sheer energy of the sector, became clear from the quality of submissions' (Ford, 1998). The shortlist included Sequence1 (1997) cast and slumped glass by Galia Amsel, as shown in Figure 6.10.

Contemporary cylinder glass

At the National Glass Centre Sunderland, designed by architect Andy Gollifer, the production of blown cylinder glass has been re-established by Sunderland Glass Works Ltd. They produce coloured and multi-layered glass by this process. 'A very large bubble is blown from a lump of glass, a 'gather', of about 8 kg. This requires a very strong highly skilled glass blower. The bubble is blown and rolled in a trough until it is about 300 mm in diameter and about 600 mm long. Then the end is cut off. It is split down one side and flattened out in a special kiln' (Rawson, 1999). A sheet of approximately 900 × 600 mm can be produced by this method. If you are frustrated by the uniformity of glass from the float process perhaps you should consider this method, which can produce glass 'of jewel like radiance' (Rawson, 1999). However, remember its relative fragility.

Polished plate

Again, this may be considered arcane. However, it was used to produce the glass for the Louvre Pyramid designed by Architect I. M. Pie and Partners with specialist input from Rice Francis Ritchie. I. M. Pie and his design team had a vision of transparency for the courtyards of this historic building and a transparency that

Figure 6.11 Cylinder glass production.

Figure 6.12 Louvre Pyramid
designed by architect I. M. Pie
and Partners.

would be maintained through two surfaces of the pyramid. The green cast of a normal sand soda lime glass, as a result largely of iron oxide impurities, was considered unacceptable. A water white glass was produced by using a specialist sand from Fontainebleau; the glass was transported to Pilkington in St Helens, England for polishing.

Edge quality and working

Annealed glass can be cut, drilled, ground and polished. If toughened glass is to be used, any edge working should be carried out prior to toughening. Edge working laminated glass can be difficult due to the edge of the laminate. Care should be taken in edge working glass to ensure that shelling is not caused, which

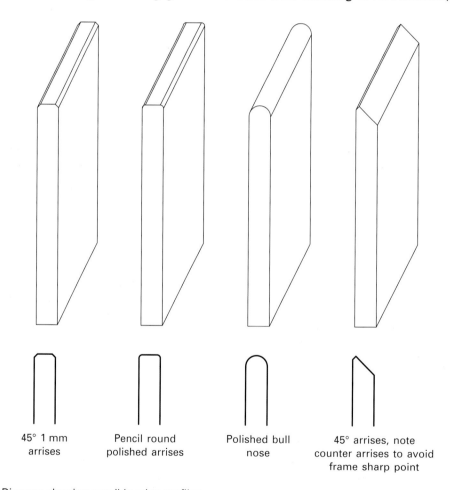

| 45° 1 mm arrises | Pencil round polished arrises | Polished bull nose | 45° arrises, note counter arrises to avoid frame sharp point |

Figure 6.13 Diagram showing possible edge profiles.

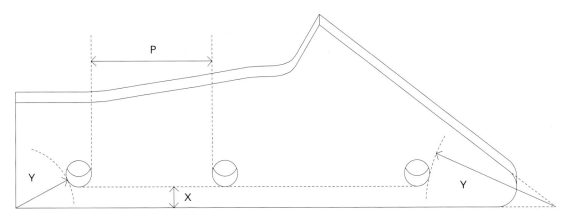

Figure 6.14 Design guidance on hole position in glass (courtesy of GGF).

Hole diameter (mm)	Minimum distance [as a value of thickness (t)]		
	P	Y	X
Up to 30 mm	4t	4t	1.5t
Over 30 mm	consult manufacturer	consult manufacturer	one third of plate width

Where:
P is the distance between adjacent holes.
X is the distance between the edge of a hole and the edge of a plate.
Y is the distance between the edge of a hole and an adjacent corner.
t is the thickness of the glass.

could lead to premature failure. Figure 6.13 shows readily available edge profiles. Although other shapes can be worked into the glass not all can be toughened.

CNC water jet cutting is now used by some suppliers to improve the positional tolerance of holes and of the sheet itself.

Glass size

The primary production process controls the potential maximum size of sheet. The current maximum width is produced by the float process. This is governed by the size of float tank, which is currently 3500 mm, although a width of 4000 mm is a future possibility being investigated by Pilkington. Each secondary process will also affect the maximum specifiable size. Producers of laminated

Table 6.2 *Available size of toughened glass from specific suppliers*

Glass type	Sheet size (mm)	Thickness (mm)	Supplier
Toughened	4200 × 2000	4–19	Pilkington
	4500 × 2100	4–25	Kite Glass
	4000 × 1600	3–25	Firman
	2000 × 1100	4	Glaverbel
	2000 × 1700	6	Glaverbel
	2000 × 3500	6–12	Glaverbel
	5000 × 2500	3–25	Solaglas
	3490 × 2800	8,10,12	St Gobain
	4500 × 2140	4–19	Bischoff Glastechnik
	7000 × 1700	4–19	Bischoff Glastechnik

glass have standardized to a maximum of 6000 × 3210 mm, known as 'float sized' laminate. This not only has advantages for the architect wanting a large area of uninterrupted glazing, but the stocking of 'float sized' laminate has led to a reduction in waste by stockists.

With laminated glass the three primary limiting factors influencing the glass size are: the size of the laminate sheet, the lamination press, and the cutting tables. For toughened glass the limitation in size is predominately a factor of the toughening furnace. There is a great diversity of sizes, representing the investment made by each company at diverse times. Table 6.2 provides the current maximum sizes for main European suppliers. It is very likely that in the near

Figure 6.15 Mechanical handling of a large double glazed unit (courtesy of Stoakes Systems).

future there will be further investment, and a toughening oven capable of at least 'float sized' toughened glass will be produced.

Once other secondary processes are introduced, further dimensional limitations or design constraints can be encountered, which relate to the mechanics of each process. The application of ceramic frit is limited by the size of the screen printing frames. Acid etching is controlled by the maximum size of bath or booth available. Low-emissivity and other sputtered coatings are limited by the size of coating chambers; a typical low-E coating will pass through five chambers. The maximum size of a double glazed unit incorporating interstitial blinds is limited by the physical constraints of assembly and transportation. The primary challenge is safely installing the blind in the air gap of the unit.

The constraint of safe handling on site has largely been overcome by mechanical handling systems, which are potential safer and require less skilled operatives (Figure 6.15).

Merlin lazer gauge

One of the problems facing an architect or engineer on site is the problem of correctly identifying the glass. Is it as specified? Symbols such as kite marks can provide only limited information, confirming that a glass is a safety glass to BS 6206, for example. It can be difficult to tell whether a double-glazing unit has the specified coating, particularly if a neutral or clear low-E coating should be present. This problem can be overcome by the use of devices such as the Merlin Lazer Gauge without the need to remove the pane or unit. This gauge measures the thickness of the glass and the thickness of the air gap in double or triple glazed units. It also identifies laminated glass and coatings on the glass, indicating on which surface the coating is. This is particularly important to ensure that a coated double glazed unit is installed the correct way round. The Merlin Lazer Gauge offers a non-destructive inspection method for checking installed glazing.

Curved glass

Glass returns to a plastic state when it is heated to about 630–690°C and it can therefore be curved and doubly curved. Doubly curved glass tends to be restricted to large run production, such as car windscreens where there is a beneficial trade-off between glass thickness and weight and the structural stiffness created by curvature. Doubly curved toughened glass was used by Nick Derbyshire on the Ticket Office/Travel Centre of Newcastle Station, manufactured by Triplex.

149

The primary methods of curving glass are:

- slump forming
- press forming
- roller hearth forming.

Slump forming is used by Romag Security Laminates and roller hearth forming by Saint Gobain-Solaglas. Slump forming, or sag bending, is used by Romag to produce curved sheets, which are then laminated into safety or security glazing, which is its specialism. Romag's maximum size is 2900 × 1950 mm with a drop or cordal height of 500 mm. The advantage of the roller hearth method is that it can be directly combined with the toughening process, resulting in curved toughened glass in one operation. Saint Gobain-Solaglas can produce a maximum size of 3650 × 2130 mm. The curved toughened glass of the Thames Water Tower was produced by Interglass.

Figure 6.16 Saint Gobain-Solaglas roller-hearth curves and toughens glass in one process.

Fire rated glazing

If you require fire rated glazing, the choice is governed by whether you need integrity only or integrity and insulation. There are three types of glass that are tested to provided integrity in a fire and will contain the smoke of the fire but not the effects of radiation:

- Georgian wired glass, or as Pilkington now name it 'Pyroshield'
- borosilicate glass, such as Pyran
- intumescent laminate glass, such as Pyrodur.

Figure 6.17 Detail of Thames Water Tower by Brookes Stacey Randall.

The latter also provides partial protection against the transmission of heat.

The stability of Georgian wired glass is the result of the electrically welded steel wires embedded in the glass. The presence of these wires has two disadvantages: one, it actually reduces the overall strength of the glass, and two, they are unsightly. Although arguably in some circumstances they manifest the presence of the glass.

In a borosilicate glass a significant proportion of the formulation of the glass is replaced by boric acid. Strangely, borosilicate glass can have a higher percentage of sodium oxide than soda lime glass. This boric acid based chemistry results in a glass with a higher chemical resistance and a lower coefficient of thermal expansion, yet it can still be heat toughened. Originally developed as a glass for chemical apparatus and gas lamp chimneys, it was introduced as fire resistant kitchenware in the 1920s. Fire resistant flat borosilicate was not introduced into buildings until the 1970s. Schott operates the worlds only float line dedicated to the production of borosilicate glasses in Jena, Germany.

If you require fire rated glazing that provides stability, integrity and insulation, there are two generic options:

- intumescent laminate glass, such as Pyrodur and Pyrostop, which can be single or double-glazed
- double glazed units with an intumescent cavity gel.

The interlayer of Pyrostop is primarily inorganic and based on silicates. It is the presence of water that causes the layer to intumese and expand when subject to heat. This also causes the interlayer to turn white and opaque, providing resistance to thermal transmission. Cavity gel intumescent glass works on a similar principle forming a white opaque resistant core when exposed to heat. A unit 18 mm thick weighs 50 kg/m^2, a significant design factor for the framing system, which must also maintain its stability, integrity and insulation during the required period of fire resistance. This form of intumescent glazing protects the fire escape stairs of the headquarters of the Hong Kong and Shanghai Bank.

When specifying fire resistant glazing it is essential to only use fully tested products and to ensure there is no substitution of even apparently incidental components that may invalidate the test data. It is also essential that the test is relevant to your proposed application. For example, most fire tests on glazing systems are vertical and not at an angle or horizontal where the self-weight of the sagging glass could have a significant effect. If you require fire rated horizontal glazing ensure it has been or is tested in that mode. It is salient to also note that BS 467 does not specifically include a test method for horizontal fire rated glazing.

Frameless fire rated glazing

Until 1998 if you required fire rated glazing it was essential to use a framework, typically of steel or hardwood, to support the glass as it softened because of the heat of the fire, and it was essential that is was thoroughly tested. In that year Schott working with Sealmaster launched a frameless fire rated glazing that uses an intumescent seal between each pane. The glass, Pyran S, spans floor to ceiling; the head and bases are secured in channels, with a minimum cover of 15–20 mm. The maximum size of pane is 3000 × 1600 mm. Pyran S is a heat toughened glass and therefore a Class A safety glass to BS 6062. As it is a borosilicate-based glass it has a low coefficient of thermal expansion, about one-third of that of soda lime glass. This system has been tested to BS 476 part 22 and offers a minimum fire rating of 30 min, stability and integrity only. Schott have successfully tested its frameless system to just under 1 hour and anticipate achieving 1 hour.

On 23 April 1999 Charles Henshaw and Sons successfully tested at Warrington Fire Research a butt-jointed assembly of clear fire rated glass to BS 476 part 22 1987. This had an overall size of 2520 mm high by 2980 mm wide. This achieved over 1 hour:63 min integrity and 63 min insulation by using 21, thick 'Pryostop', an insulating glass manufactured by Pilkington. The maximum pane size tested was 2400 mm high and 1400 mm wide; the butt joint was formed from 'clear' mastic.

Development of countersunk fittings

Compare, for example, a countersunk fitting for single and double glazing with the substantial brass plates used to retain the toughened glass walling of Wills

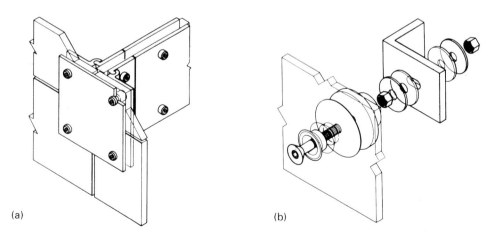

(a)   (b)

Figure 6.18 Comparison of (a) 165 × 165 patch plate and (b) countersunk 'mark one' Planar fitting.

Faber Dumas building, Ipswich, by Foster Associates in 1973. Four brass patch plates, 165 × 165 mm and manufactured by Newman Tonks, secure the toughened glass back to internal glass fins and the total assembly is suspended from the concrete slab of the roof.

Within 10 years, Pilkington had reduced the means of securing toughened glass to a flush countersunk machine screw fitting of 28 mm external diameter. The result was a frameless and visually uninterrupted facade of glass as transparent as the chosen glass. The fitting was first used on Briarcliff House, Farnborough (by Arup Associates) and the Renault Centre (by Foster Associates). On the latter building the fitting was also used to support frameless roof lights. At this stage the fitting was simply known as a 901 mark 1. The precursor of this fitting is believed to be a countersunk fitting developed for the glazed rear walls of squash courts.

Although developed to produce flush uninterrupted facades, the fitting, now know as Planar, has an expressive and constructive quality. Each pane is bolted to the building, and there is a clear separation of skin, fixings and structure. Since its introduction in 1981 the fitting has been refined to a neat, machined stainless assembly tightened by discrete pins, the 902. Double-glazed Planar was first used on the Porsche UK Headquarters, Reading (by Dewhurst Haslam Partnership) in the form of almost 4° rooflights. Pilkington found it necessary to introduce a diamond-shaped back plate, which replaced the inner pane of the sealed double glazed unit, enabling a standard Planar fitting to be fixed to the outer pane.

Pilkington promptly developed a countersunk through fixing for double-glazing. It is salient to note that Pilkington did not patent the concept of Planar, however they did patent the double glazed fitting. Although Pilkington has now developed a transparent spacer for double glazed Planar, and despite the same flush external quality as its single glazed counterpart, it does not have the same minimalism and transparency of detailing. This is because of the need to introduce an extruded aluminium edges section, which also contains desiccant, and this is sealed to the glass with a combination of butyl and silicone, both of which are black.

There is now a range of countersunk fittings that can be specified. Some were developed for specific projects, such as the fitting developed for Parc de La Villete by Rice Francis Ritchie and Greenburg, which was then marketed by SIV. Some fittings are direct commercial rivals of Planar and this includes Hansen. All the fittings share the need to 'soften' the contact between the bolt and the glass of the countersunk hole. In Planar this is achieved by a shaped 'nylatron' polyamide washer, and at Parc de La Villete it is achieved by a formed aluminium washer. The generic difference between these two fittings is the way they seek to minimize bending stress in the glass. Pilkington use a combination of silicone

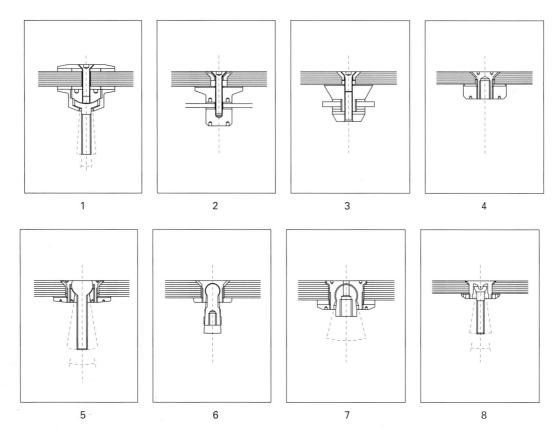

Figure 6.19 Bolted fixings available to secure toughened glass.
1. Circular patch fitting – Marcus Summers Solaglas Saint Gobain
2. Pilkington Planar 902 mark 2 countersunk fitting
3. Greenberg Hansen G10
4. Eckelt Litewall
5. Structawall 2
6. SIV – developed from RFR's fitting for Parc de la Villette Bioclamatic Facades
7. Solaglas Saint Gobain countersunk fitting (± 5° angular rotation)
8. Sitbra fitting for canopy of Funiculaire de Montmartre (± 22° angular rotation)

washers and flexibility in the supporting bracket or casting. Originally, Pilkington called these components spring plates. Pilkington's approach is primarily based on material science whereas Peter Rice and colleague chose a more 'mathematical' approach, one that was readily analysed by introducing a spherical bearing into the plane of the glass. Clearly this is a more expensive fitting but the approach has been followed by GEM Belgium and by Eckelt.

Specifying Planar is unlike other forms of curtain walling because it is not necessarily the specialist subcontractor that is responsible for the visual and detailed appearance of the assembly. The interface between the bolted fixing and the supporting structure is of particular importance.

Glass as a structural component

The combination of physical testing experience with the sharing of knowledge has been critical to the rapid development of glass as a structural component in the last 30 years. The experience gained from one project has been taken and extended onto the next. Paradoxically, the increased emphasis on safety regulations has been a stimulus and not an inhibitor, as it has tended to draw together the one-off project and the available mass market techniques. There are still no codes of practice for the use of glass as a structural material and many innovations were developed on modestly sized projects.

Figure 6.20 All-glass house designed by the author.

Glass House 1982

This was a competition entry design by the author in 1982. The enclosure and structure of the house were formed from clear toughened glass as a folded plate structure. The cross-section is a rigid portal frame describing a rectilinear geometry. The house was environmentally sound, although 100% glass above ground. The inner leaf of the glass structure had a clear hard low-emissivity coating and air was drawn through this double layer providing cooling or heating as necessary. A very low air infiltration rate was achieved and heat reclaim units were proposed as part of the air handling system. The thermal mass of the foundation was an intrinsic part of the thermal balance of the design. The house was envisaged as a family home that could be readily built with the existing urban and suburban fabric. Countersunk fitting were used as 'fail safe ties' between the folded plate elements.

Figure 6.21 Sonsbeek Pavilion (architect Bentham and Crouwel with engineers ABT).

Sonsbeek Pavilion 1986

This glass pavilion was designed by architects Bentham and Crouwel, with Robert Nissje of engineers ABT, to house some of the more delicate structures in that year's exhibition entitled 'Skin'. Although a temporary pavilion (it was dismantled in October 1996) it was designed as a permanent structure at the request of the Dutch regulatory authorities. The structurally glazed pavilion gently stepped down the slope in four sections. The structure of the pavilion comprised 580 mm deep 15 mm thick toughened glass fins, which supported 600 mm deep steel trusses, which spanned the 6.2 m width of the pavilion. The trusses comprised back to back angles with 20 mm diameter, steel rod diagonal members. The 18 mm laminated roof glazing bore directly onto the steel trusses via a 10 mm thick polyurethane pad. The weathering joint of the roof glazing was silicone sealed and was also silicone sealed to the truss. At the changes of

Figure 6.22 Detail of the Sonsbeek Pavilion showing the truss glass mullion and wall connection.

level the truss was left open to provide ventilation. The 10 mm clear toughened glass walls were hung from two bolted fixings at the end of each truss with an external patch plate. All clamped details were separated by 2.5 mm thick felt pads. Robert Nissje advised that 'the longitudinal stability was provided by the glass wall plates connected by silicone joints'.[3] The startling transparency of this pavilion was a source of controversy and inspiration. Peter Buchanan (1987) writing in the Architectural Review (1987) suggested the 'emperor has no cloths'.

Rick Mather – Hampstead Extension 1992

By 1992, technology and courage had come together and were realized in the modest form of an all-glass extension to a house in Hampstead by architect Rick Mather and engineer Tim Macfarlane. The steel beams were omitted and by adapting principles from timber construction an all-glass construction achieved. Apparently the client is a high court judge yet this did not inhibit the design team.

Tim Macfarlane mused that 'Rick Mather Architects kept asking if we could make the structural steel member smaller and smaller. In a fit of either inspiration or exasperation, I suggested using beams of laminated glass instead of steel! We were apprehensive about using a single pane of toughened glass for the beams supporting the horizontal load of the roof because toughened glass could easily break, so we decided to laminate three panes of glass tougher for optimum

[3]Robert Nissje, Lecture at Architectural Association, London, 1993.

safety. Even if all three of these beams were to break, the crack pattern in the annealed glass would ensure that the glass stuck to the PVB and did not fall down and cause injury. Laminated glass thereby acts as a true fail safe solution' (DuPont, 1998). The glass beams are joined to the glass plate columns by a tenon joint with the glass fin being trapped between the two outer layers of the glass beam. The double glazed walls are also remarkable for two reasons: they have transparent spacer bars, and a sputtered metallic coating which acts as an electrical heat source when a current is applied. Thus maximum transparency is achieved and down draft is avoided. To achieve this the glass was coated in Finland and the double glazed units were produced in Germany and then transported to London.

Figure 6.23 Hampstead Extension (architect Rick Mather with engineers Dewhurst Macfarlane).

Glass Bridge for Kraayanvanger Urbis 1994

Robert Nijsse was asked by architects Kraayvanger Urbis of Rotterdam to participate in the design of a bridge for their own offices. Robert Nijsse found that 'an architect as client was a very helpful circumstance'. The bridge is an all-glass assembly, which exploits the properties of float, laminate, and toughened glass to form a connection between two buildings 3 m up in the air. The glass is clear so colleagues meeting here by chance are held almost effortlessly in space. The floor beams are three layers of 10 mm float with 0.76 mm PVB interlayers. The floor comprises two layers of 15 mm float laminated with 0.76 mm PVB interlayer.

Figure 6.24 Detail of the Hampstead Extension: tenon detail at the junction of the glass mullion and glass roof beam.

Figure 6.25 Glass Bridge for Kraayanvanger Urbis (engineer Robert Nijsse of ABT).

The walls and roof glass comprise 10 mm toughened laminated with 0.76 mm PVB interlayer to an inner layer of heat strengthened glass, which also has sputtered low emissivity coating. This bridge took 6 months from design to completion, but it only took 2 days to erect it on site!

Tokyo International Forum Canopy 1996

Tim Macfarlane noted that 'The structural problems posed by Rafael Viñoly's dream of an all-glass cantilever canopy for the Yurakucho subway station entrance in Tokyo International Forum took us 6 to 7 months to solve' (DuPont, 1998). The complete process from initial enquiry to completion took almost 1 year, a remarkably short period of time given the level of invention, rigor and persuasion required to realize this project. A 10.6 m cantilevering entrance canopy all in glass was achieved by using layered laminated beam which were bolted together to form the long span elements. These beams support the laminated glass panes, which also brace the structure. The design of this canopy is an engaging journey from an initial sketch on a restaurant napkin, through 1:20 scale models, to the realization in Tokyo. Firman produced the profiled and laminated glass beams in London.

The key component of the canopy is the layered and overlapping profiled glass beams and the stainless steel bezel, which transmits load evenly from the beam.

Tim Macfarlane's concept for the bezel and glass beam was initially tested on a 'crude' rig at Firman, capable of carrying 6 tonnes. This was followed by the testing of a small sample with bezel and pins at Imperial College London, followed by the testing of a full size beam. The assembly successfully sustained a breaking load of 11 tonnes.

The canopy is erected in an earthquake zone and therefore the safety was critical. Unfortunately despite the test of laminated glass beam to a wind pressure equivalent to 5 tonnes, the Metropolitan Government of Tokyo insisted that acrylic sheet be added as an additional 'fail safe', a belt and braces approach that potentially reduced the transparency realized. The completed canopy, however, remains a tour de force of transparency and constructional clarity. The root of the beam comprises seven layers comprising 19 mm laminated glass and 19 mm acrylic sheet. The layering diminishes in five stages as the cantilever

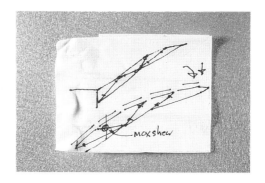

Figure 6.26 Sketch of Tokyo International Forum Canopy by Tim Macfarlane.

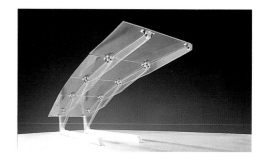

Figure 6.27 Model of Tokyo International Forum Canopy.

Figure 6.28 Tokyo International Forum Canopy (architect Rafael Viñoly engineer Dewhurst Macfarlane).

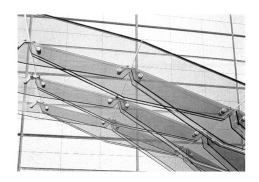

Figure 6.29 Detail of Tokyo International Forum Canopy showing the bezels connecting the layered glass and acrylic fins.

extends, ending in a single blade of 19 mm laminated glass. The layering of the beam relates directly to the roof modules, which also comprise two 19 mm sheets of laminated glass.

20 m Spanning all-glass bridge 1999

This long span yet all-glass bridge is the vision of artist Thomas Heatherwick working with engineer Anthony Hunt Associates. The proposal is to use 19 mm thick sheets of glass, which are trapezoidal, nominally 500 mm deep by 1000 mm, to form a facetted arch, thus forming the deck and structure of the bridge achieving a span of 20 m. The design team aims to progress from the 1:50 model displayed at the 1999 Royal Academy Summer Exhibition to built examples. The current limiting factor is not the glass; it is the lack of a truly transparent

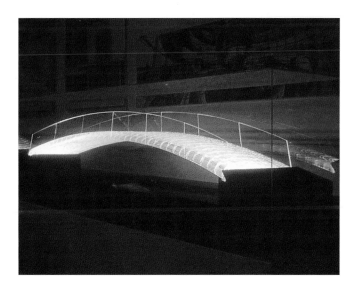

Figure 6.30 Model of a proposed 20 m span all-glass bridge displayed at the Royal Academy Summer Show 1999 (artist Thomas Heatherwick with engineer Anthony Hunt Associates).

adhesive. Anthony Hunt Associates are developing appropriate transparent bonding agents with adhesive and surface specialists.

Glass stairs

Paul Scheerbart in his Glasarchitektur 1914 envisioned a 'glass architecture, which lets in the light of the sun, the moon and stars, not merely through a few windows but through every possible wall, which will be made entirely of glass'. Note that when he wrote this, toughened glass was little more than a theoretical possibility, laminated glass had been invented and large plate production had begun. Architecture and engineering possibly appear to be painfully slow moving professions, and yet now it is possible to make walls, roofs, and floors of glass. The glass stair, that transportation of delight in space, is perhaps the perfect embodiment of Scheerbart's dream.

Glass Stairs: Eva Jiricna

Figure 6.31 illustrates examples of the many glass and stainless steel staircases designed by Eva Jiricna Associates. She has with her colleagues developed a rich language and grammar of staircase design, with as much emphasis on the potential of surface pattern on or in the glass as its transparency. The staircase design for Joseph Ettedgui in 1986–88, for his eponymously named shop at 77 Fulham Road, London, was suspended from the first floor on stainless steel rods. Sadly, it is currently in storage. The glass treads are backed up by acrylic sheet of equal thickness. This in turn is stiffened by small, stainless steel push-rod trusses. The assembly described by Peter Davey (1989) as 'a brightly lit and glittering cage', uses a highly consistent assembly of bolted stainless steel rods to link the treads and the suspension system.

The spiral staircase at Joan and David, Bond Street, London is less gravity-defying with a central curved core of coated mild steel from which stainless steel tripods reach out to support the treads, again a combination of glass and acrylic. Here the treads are manifest by a strong etched diagonal pattern. The balustrade is formed of carefully aligned curved clear toughened glass, which presents a simple foil to the stair itself. Even if one does not share the almost baroque sensibility of Eva Jiricna, these stairs promote delight and wonderment.

Glass Stair Lowe Apartment 1996

Brookes Stacey Randall's spatial concept of the Lowe Apartment was to retain the maximum sense of space, whilst accommodating all the needs of modern

Figure 6.31 (a) Staircase at Joseph Shop, Sloane Street. (b) Detail of the staircase at Joseph Shop, Sloane Street. (c) Staircase of the house in Rutland Gate, Knightsbridge. (d) Detail of the staircase of the house in Rutland Gate. (All by architect Eva Jiricna Associates).

Figure 6.32 Glass stair of the Lowe Apartment by Brookes Stacey Randall.

urban life, from sleeping to home office, from relaxing to cooking to entertaining friends. The bed space was therefore conceived as a mezzanine suspended in space and the stair to it should interrupt the flow of space as little as possible. As Nik Randall stated 'our aim was to make the stair simply beautiful'. The design of the stair was developed with Tim Macfarlane and a prototype tested at Oxford University (see Figure 7.8, Chapter 7).

The glass treads and risers form a stiff folded plate structure, which forms the cords of a truss between two 20 mm diameter stainless steel rods. The connection between the rods and the glass is made by a stainless steel lost wax casting. Note the stop end casting on the first and last treads. The casting

Figure 6.33 Detail of the glass stair at the Lowe Apartment.

Figure 6.34 Glass stair of the Art House. Architect Brookes Stacey Randall.

is fixed to the glass via conical stainless steel 'pig nosed' fixings in nylon sleeves. It is these fixings that lock the structure together. The treads and risers are formed from two sheets of toughened clear glass laminated together with a cold curing acrylic resin, which is approximately 1 mm thick. The two sheets of glass forming each tread and riser are 10 and 12 mm thick; they are of different thicknesses as this was the structural minimum and more economical.

Brookes Stacey Randall has extended the concept of the stair for Chris Lowe's apartment for the Art House project in Chelsea. Here the stair is wider and rises up two stories and has clear glass balustrades. It is accompanied by a smaller bridge-like glass stair, which links two mezzanines.

Figure 6.35 Detail of glass stair of the Art House.

Further information

BSEN 572	Glass in Building. Basic soda lime silicate glass products (parts 1–7) e.g. part 2: Float glass
BS 5713	Specification for hermetically sealed flat double glazing units
BS 6206	Specification for impact performance requirements for flat safety glass and safety plastics for use in buildings
BS 6262	Code of practice for glazing for buildings
prEN 1279	Glass in building – insulating glass units
BSEN 1863	Glass in building – heat strengthened glass
BSEN 12150	Glass in building – thermally toughened safety glass
BSEN 12337	Glass in building – chemical strengthened glass
BSENISO 12543	Glass in building – laminated glass and laminated safety glass (parts 1–6)
prEN 12725	Glass in building – glass block walls dimensions and performance
prEN 12758-1	Glass in building – glazing and airborne sound insulation: Part 1 Definitions and determination of properties
DIN 18516	Part 4 Standard for heat soaking toughened glass

References

Brookes, A.J. and Greck, C. (1992). *Connections*. Butterworth-Heinemann.

Buchanan, P. (1987). 'Barely There' *Architectural Review*, Vol. 182, No. 1087, The Architectural Press, September.

Button, D. and Pye, B. (eds) (1993). *Glass in Building*. Butterworth, p. 213.

Davey, P. (1989). 'Jimena Bravura' *Architectural Review*. Vol. CLXXXV, No. 1103, The Architectural Press, pp. 36–40.

Dawson, S. (1997). Glass breaks a new barrier, in *The Architects Journal,* Vol. 205, No. 1, pp. 37–39.

Dawson, S. (1998). Glass goes round the bend, in *The Architects Journal,* Vol. 208, No. 4, pp. 42–44.

DuPont (1998). Butacite Laminate Glass News, Issue 9: p. 3.

Eekhout, M. (ed.) (1992). *The Glass Envelope*. Conference Papers TU Delft.

Elliot, C. (1992). *Technics and Architecture*. MIT Press.

Ford, T. (1998). Introduction to the Jerwood Prize. *Applied Art 1998: Glass Catalogue*. The Craft Council.

GGF Glazing Manual. Glass and Glazing Federation (on going)

Jofeh, C. (1999). *Structural Use of Glass*. Institute of Structural Engineers.

Rawson, J. (1996). Shedding light on glass. *The Architects Journal* vol: 47.

Rawson, J. (1999). Window of opportunity. *The Architects Journal* vol: 36.

Rice, P. (1994). *An Engineer Imagines*. Artemis.

Wilkinson, C. (1992). *Supersheds*. Butterworth-Heinemann.

Wigginton, M. (1996). *Glass in Architecture*. Phaidon.

7

Prototypes and testing

'There is nothing mysterious in the process of innovation. What is needed is just courage, care and attention to detail, and above all belief and getting started' (Peter Rice, 1994)

If you have the desire or need to innovate, your vision of a particular assembly cannot be sourced from off the shelf components. It is essential that at the earliest possible stage you establish that the assembly is viable, will perform, and is visually satisfactory. This is best achieved through a process of samples, mock-ups, prototypes, and testing. The role in a design development process, of ideas communicated via sketches, drawing and discussions, cannot be overstated. The use of computer modelling helps to inform this process and can facilitate the production of prototypes. Renzo Piano describes how the use of physical models returns his thinking to the artisan or constructive

Figure 7.1 Peter Rice at Park de La Villette.

process, however large and political the project. The use of physical testing has led some architects to work in a manner that is closer to the nineteenth century engineers such as Brunel or Turner. The knowledge and confidence gained by testing is incomparable, even in an era of computer-generated computation and virtual reality. Research, design and development are a route to minimize risk, providing reliability and certainty, and resulting in a robust constructional technology.

Testing

As in the design process itself the starting point for a test, or programme of tests, is to establish the range of performance criteria to be met and thus the nature of testing required.

There are seven primary types of tests:

- holistic testing of building assemblies, i.e. fire or weather tests
- subassembly tests, i.e. cyclic loading
- component tests, i.e. load or fatigue
- quality control testing, i.e. bond quality or chemical composition
- coupon test, to establish mechanical characteristics
- site-based tests, i.e. concrete cube or screed strength
- testing for durability and serviceability, i.e. long-term exposure to UV light.

It may be critical to the overall economic viability of a component or assembly to establish whether non-destructive test methods are available, and the cost of the testing process. If the testing is for a one-off project, the need for testing should be established at an early stage and included in the project specification; for example, in the performance specification of the glazed assembly. Historically the building industry has carried out too little testing and in particular too few holistic tests of building assemblies. Good examples of holistic testing are:

- weather
- fire
- structural frames
- acoustic.

Weather testing

Curtain wall, cladding and glazing assemblies are best tested off site using a recognized test method; BS 5368 Parts 1–3, is the norm for steady-state weather testing. It is now harmonized with European Standards as EN42, EN86 and EN77, respectively. Although the test method contained in BS 5368 is for windows, it is now widely applied to curtain wall, cladding, and glazing assemblies. This test method establishes the ability of an assembly to sustain wind loading, its air leakage rate, and its resistance to rain penetration. The test rig is calibrated and the set cycle undertaken. The sample is loaded progressively by the application of air pressure or suction to simulate wind load; deflections at agreed location are monitored using transducers. Air leakage is recorded at this stage. The water jets are turned on and the assembly is monitored for leakage up to the specified wind pressure. The norm for water resistance in Britain is that there shall be no leakage when the assembly is tested at 600 Pa. The wind load is removed and the complete cycle repeated. At the end of the test the assembly is inspected as it is disassembled. Clearly if the test is successful, any modifications carried out to achieve this result must be incorporated in the final product or project assembly. The Centre for Window and Curtain Walling Technology (CWCT) in its Standard and Guide to Good Practice

Curtain Walling recommend the use of a modified version of BS 5368, in particular, it uses a higher volume of water.

The size of test sample is usually governed by two criteria: the size of the components specified, and the test centre used. Three of the leading test centres in the UK are: British Standards Institute (BSI) at Hemel Hempstead, Building Research Establishment (BRE) at Cardington, and Taywood Engineering at Southall. BSI's rigs are internal and its current maximum is a test assembly 4500 mm wide by 3400 mm high. BSI offers the advantage of a controlled 'warehouse' environment. Taywood Engineering's test rigs are external and thus larger. Its current maximum sizes are 13 m wide × 10 m high and 7 m wide × 18 m high. The latter test was for Planar curtain wall, designed and manufactured by Pilkington Archi-

Figure 7.2 Aspect 2 cladding system undergoing a BS 5368 weather test at BSI.

tectural for LG Kangnam Tower in Seoul, Korea. This rig was weather tested to BS 5368 Parts 1–3 and also underwent a seismic load test. This was achieved by use of hydraulic rams simulating the loading that the facade would experience in an earthquake. Taywood Engineering are willing to extend their rigs as may be necessary for a particular building or product development. It has also established a second test centre at Al Abbar, Dubai.

Figure 7.3 Glazing system of East Croydon Station being tested to BS 5368 Parts 1–3 at Taywood Engineering.

Figure 7.4 Prototypical concrete frame undergoing testing by BRE at their Cardington Shed.

Rainscreen cladding can be tested to BS 5368 Parts 1–3; however, the full back-up wall needs to be present and the criteria of success and failure agreed at the outset. For example, how much water penetration is permissible into the interstitial cavity, and whether potential wetting of the insulation layer is acceptable.

Some specialists argue that the test method stated in BS 5368 does not sufficiently replicate the dynamic loading of wind on buildings, which can change rapidly and be both positive and negative. It is this rapid reversal of loading, which combined with rain, tests whether the seals of an assembly can withstand exposure without leakage. Arguably a pressure equalized curtain walling assembly can only be fully tested via a dynamic test.

The Architectural Aluminium Manufacturers Association standard AAMA 501.183 test is based on the use of dynamic pressure, generated by an aero-engine and

Figure 7.5 European dynamic weather test, prEn 13050.

propeller set. Taywood Engineering and BRE have been instrumental in the development of a draft European weather test, pr En 13050. In part, the aim was to standardize the dynamic testing across Europe. Where the AAMA test uses an aero-engine, which is difficult to calibrate across a number of test centres, the new European test uses a fan of known and repeatable performance. This fan travels across the facade assembly being tested on a mechanized gantry. One criticism of this test method is the relatively small area of the fan, which works well on curtain walling but is too small to test rainscreen cladding effectively. An alternative static test method is BSEN 12155; see the Further Information section at the end of this chapter for its companion tests.

Fire testing

The Construction Products Directive is intended to remove barriers to trade between members of the European Union. This is leading to a harmonization of standards throughout its member states. However, building regulations remain the responsibility of national governments and therefore a product could be tested to a harmonized European Standard and yet not be acceptable in the context of the building regulations of a specific nations building regulations. The prefix prEN indicates that a standard is going through the process of standardization at CEN. Fire testing is an example of the harmonization of test methods and related standards. The Fire Research Station of BRE has a key role in this process, from a United Kingdom perspective.

At Borehamwood, the Loss Prevention Council of United Kingdom, now part of BRE, has carried out a set of holistic fire tests on curtain walling assemblies up to 10 m high. LPC's principal interest was to investigate the way in which glass curtain walling performs in a fire and the effectiveness of the design of fire stops at each structural slab level. Generally the fire was generated with a polypropylene crib of timber.

Warrington Fire Research Establishment is another leading fire test centre in the United Kingdom. RAPRA has independent fire test laboratories, which specialize in the fire testing of plastics, natural rubber and synthetic elastomers, foams and polymer products.

Figure 7.6 Snoopy fire test at BRE.

Acoustic testing

Testing the acoustic performance of modular internal partitions has been long established, having been set out in the 1950s in the Method of Building Series, Blue Book(s). However, tighter environmental noise regulations have also placed the emphasis on the need to test cladding units and external wall construction to establish the noise reduction capabilities. Taywood Engineering can test samples 3.7 m wide × 4.75 m high to ISO140 and ASTM standards. The modelling and testing of room acoustics is critical in specific building types, such as concert halls and opera houses.

Load testing

Figure 7.7 shows an impromptu load test of a concrete structure of La Jacaranda Night Club designed by Felix Candela. One-off load testing of structures is generally no longer necessary, as there are established design criteria for reinforced concrete, steel, and aluminium. The particular geometry of the proposed structure or component or the nature of the connections may prompt the need to test the use of bonded connections in a tubular aluminium assembly or a composite construction. For some materials there are, as yet, no established design criteria for their use in buildings.

Although the use of glass for floors and staircases is now well-established (see chapter 6) testing may prove necessary to verify the load capacity and to satisfy Building Control if there is no normative standard to work to. The test carried out on a prototype for the stair at Chris Lowe's apartment, designed by Brookes Stacey Randall with engineer Dewhurst Macfarlane, focused on the folded plate structure of laminated toughened glass. The stainless steel stringers of the completed stair (see Fig. 7.8) were replaced by mild steel tubes, and the castings by fabrications. It was the principle behind the folded glass structure which required testing, not the relatively familiar metal components.

Figure 7.7 Felix Candela – an impromptu load test of the concrete structure for La Jacaranda Night Club, Mexico, 1957.

Figure 7.8 A prototype section of the staircase for Chris Lowe's apartment being tested at Oxford University.

It can be prudent to load-test cast components to check their ability to carry the design load safely. This could be a question of the form, the chemical composition, or the integrity of the casting, for example. See Chapter 3 for further discussion of this issue.

Cyclic load testing

The role of a component or its exposure to extreme environmental conditions will result in the need for cyclic load testing. This examines the ability of the element on test to sustain repeated loading and relaxation, testing for fatigue failure, or disassembly by vibration. Figure 7.9 shows the clamping assembly of Aspect 2 cladding system being tested at Bath University. The extruded aluminium clamp, M6 stainless steel bolt and nylock successfully sustained 10 000 cycles.

Quality control testing

Many of the above tests would be one-off tests for a specific project or the development of a new component or system. Quality control testing, however, should inherently be carried out regularly during production and be logged, often requiring the recording of the environmental conditions of the factory to be recorded. Depending on the level of traceability required, individual components may need to be identified, with a non-removable code number or bar code. Often, quality control test methods are destructive.

Figure 7.9 Cyclic load testing of the clamping assembly of Aspect 2.

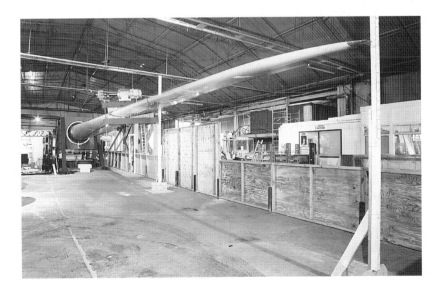

Figure 7.10 A timber composite wind generator rota arm undergoing cyclic load testing. (Courtesy of Taywood Engineering).

For example, heat-soaking of glass to test for nickel sulphide inclusions causes the vast majority of sheets with such inclusions to shatter in the factory, not on site or in use. The testing of film thickness of coatings is by a scratch test. To overcome the destruction of valuable components, one method is to introduce representative samples into each batch; this is good practice in laminated panel production. Coseley test 300 × 300 mm laminated panel samples for bond quality, and test a set number of samples per batch.

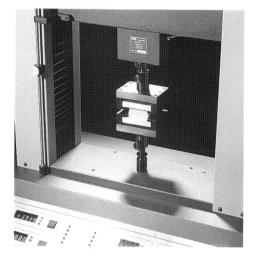

Figure 7.11 Batch quality testing of the bond quality of a composite panel.

Thermal testing

The thermal resistance or U-value of a component can be established by testing in a hot box test such as BS EN ISO 8990. However, components such as windows require additional procedures beyond this standard. The thermal performance of an existing building or a newly completed project can be checked by thermal imaging using an infra-red camera. Thermographic surveys of completed buildings are carried out by a number of organizations including BRE and BSRIA. It is also possible to analyse the performance of a building fabric, perhaps a key detail in a silicone bonded curtain walling assembly, to establish the heat loss, any cold bridging, and the risk of condensation. This computer analysis software, similar to the flow modelling used in casting design, is available as a design service from consultancies such as Sandberg Consulting Engineers (see Figure 7.12).

Prototypes

Some may question the need or time taken to prototype a component or consider it only possible on a high value project or a well-endowed design development programme. The benefits of prototyping are considerable and are not necessarily expensive or time-consuming. The prototype may be produced to test an engineering principle, the fit of a component, or to measure its aesthetic quality. Klavs Helweg-Larsen, the architect of the KTAS telephone booth illustrated in Chapter 5, used cut-out templates of the booth from a very early stage in its design. He notes that 'There are no fixed rules on how to achieve harmonic

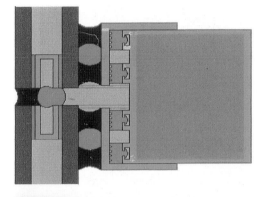

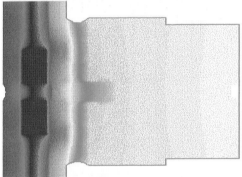

Figure 7.12 Analysis of the thermal performance of a silicone bonded glazing system prepared by Sandberg Consulting Engineers. Assessed glazing detail (top), predicted temperature contours (middle) and location of thermal bridges (bottom).

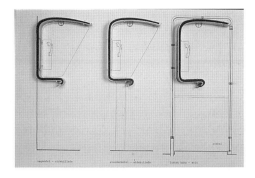

Figure 7.13 Cut-outs of variants of the KTAS telephone booth designed by Klavs Helweg-Larsen.

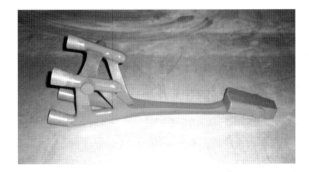

Figure 7.14 Timber prototype of the stainless steel casting for the Thames Water Tower.

proportions. Yet the difference between good and bad can be a question of a few mm' (Helweg-Larsen, 1985). Visualizing those subtle differences and modifying the end product as a result is the essence of the process of prototyping.

Rapid prototypes and digital design

Even in this digital age the fastest prototypes may be cut by hand from balsa, foam board, or Styrofoam. The breadboard model of the Dyson DCO2 vacuum

177

cleaner and the blue foam model (see Figure 7.15), vital in the design development of this product, were both produced by hand.

However, the need to develop prototypes, often in constrained timescales, to inform the design and production process (design with production) and harnessing the digital data, has (in the past 20 years) led to the development of rapid prototype techniques, to the extent that it is possible to realize 'physical desk top publishing'.

Rapid prototypes are produced from digital design files by two generic methods: subtractive or additive. The main subtractive methods are: computer numeric control (CNC) cutting-plasma, laser or water jet, three- or five-axis milling machines.

CAD CAM (computer aided design, computer aided manufacture) can be used for the production of sheet components. The digital co-ordinates of the design file are used to guide a plasma cutter, water jet cutter or punch tool, resulting in a direct replication of the architect's or designer's drawing (design file). If the final component is a flat sheet product the prototype stage can be omitted.

The digital co-ordinates can also be used to control a three- or five-axis milling machine, which will 'erode' the final form from a block of a relatively soft material such as Styrofoam.

This technique is used in the production of moulded components including acrylic baths, or carbon fibre shells and the patterns for metal castings. Although in

(a)

(b)

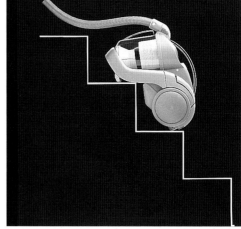

(c)

Figure 7.15 Development of the Dyson DCO2 vacuum cleaner: (a) 'breadboard' prototype; (b) foam model; (c) working prototype.

Figure 7.16 Rapid prototype of a thermal imaging camera for Marconi by Alloy. (a) CAD 3D model of the Marconi thermal imaging camera. (b) Rapid prototype foam model image of thermal imaging camera. (c) Photo realistic rendering of the thermal imaging camera.

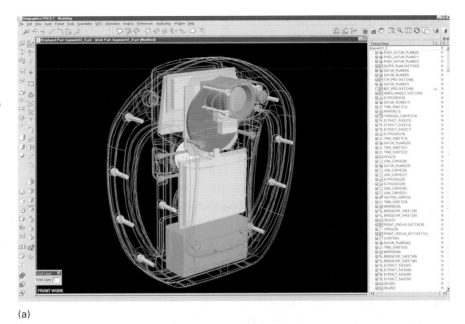

(a)

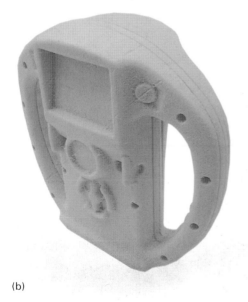

(b)

(c)

the latter category, skilled joiners are often employed for their speed and accuracy, and because of the large scale of some castings.

The additive processes available for the production of rapid prototypes include:

- steriolithography

- selective laser sintering
- fused deposition
- multi-jet modelling
- laminated object manufacture

The common characteristic of all of these processes is the incremental deposition, curing or binding of very thin layers of material in a 'build chamber'. The rapid prototyping software converts the three-dimensional computer model into very thin horizontal layers, which are built up dependant on the process (see below). The size of additive rapid prototypes (ARP) is limited by the build chamber although this can be overcome by bonding sectional parts together.

Steriolithography

The rapid prototype is built up by selectively exposing a bath of photosensitive resin to laser light. Once each layer has set, the next layer is traced until the prototype is complete. Steriolithography is used by major curtain walling companies; for example, to model proposed new extrusions at full size. It should be remembered that this demonstrates the form, not the material quality or physical properties of the final component.

This process has been commercially available since 1986, having been developed by 3D Systems of California. Because steriolithography was the pioneering form of additive rapid prototyping the computer format STL has become the predominant format used for all forms of ARP. Computer modelling software such as Form Z can export data in STL format.

Selective laser sintering

Similar in technique to steriolithography. However, laser heat, instead of laser light, is used causing specially coated grains of sand or metal to fuse together. An alternative form of sintering is the layered deposition of binder alternating with layers of granular material. Once complete, the prototype or model is dusted or vacuumed to remove excess powder.

CERAM Research, who provide technical and commercial services to the ceramics industry, has been leading a Sector Challenge-funded research programme into rapid prototyping for the ceramics industry (Anon, 1999). The rapid prototyping has been undertaken by Warwick University's Advanced Manufacturing Centre. CERAM investigated three rapid prototyping options: resin, heat bonded sheet, or fine heat fusible powder such as wax or thermoplastic. They found that heat fusible powder is best suited to ceramics, using a process called Selective

Laser Sintering. CERAM reports 'A CO_2 laser draws the CAD slices on the surface of the powder, locally melting and fusing it together. A new layer of powder is placed on top of the completed slice with a roller and the next slice is drawn. Once the model has been built, the unsintered powder around the slices is removed' (Anon, 1999). This physical prototype can then be used to evaluate the ceramic element and can be used to manufacture Plaster of Paris moulds. A mould can also be directly machined from the CAD file further shortening the design development process. The low cost of rapid prototyping 'encourages corporate commitment to creativity' (Anon, 1999). The tile manufacturer, H&R Johnson Ceramic, has found that the use of rapid prototyping has reduced its 50–day prototyping timescale to 8 days. Selective laser sintering is directly applicable to the rapid prototyping of other components such as metal castings.

Fused deposition

This is based on the deposition of a thermoplastic by a computer control head, which progressively delivers each layer. The thermoplastic sets almost immediately on delivery and fairly robust rapid prototypes can be produced.

Multi-jet modelling

A standard ink jet printer head is used to deliver a water-based binder to cellulose particles (starch) or gypsum powder, to form the digitally specified layer. Once complete, the bed of the 'build chamber' is lowered and the next layer formed.

Laminated object manufacture

This is based on two-dimensional laser cutting with the ARP being built up of bonded layers of paper. The build chamber is fed by a roller, carrying paper coated on its lower surface with adhesive. Following the application of a second layer of paper they are bonded together by a heated roller. Each layer is cut by a laser, prior to the application of the next paper layer. The completed ARP is removed from the stack of paper layers and can be sanded like wood. Dr Kevin Rotheroe notes that 'A model component can be CNC milled from wood. However, this approach is often less expensive' (Rotheroe, 2001).

Quantum cloud

Antony Gormley's sculpture entitled Quantum Cloud (Figure 7.17a) is located at Millennium Pier, North Greenwich, outside 'the Dome'. Rapid prototyping was

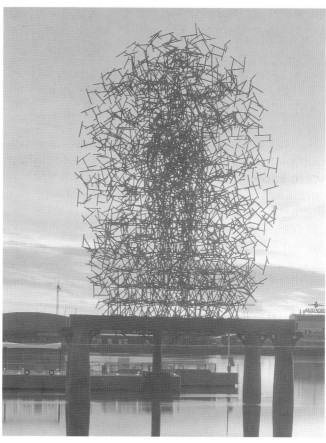

Figure 7.17 (a) Antony Gormley's sculpture entitled Quantum Cloud, North Greenwich, 1999; (b) rapid prototypes of a node for the structure of Antony Gormley's sculpture Quantum Cloud; (c) cast node for the structure of Antony Gormley's sculpture Quantum Cloud.

(a)

(b)

(c)

essential in the delivery of the sculptor's vision of a human void in a metallic cloud (see Figure 7.17).

Antony Gormley insisted that nodes of the structure were no more apparent than the rest of the structure, thus ruling out a conventional space frame node. Structural Engineer Gary Elliot noted 'the complex geometry of the primary structure, with differing angles and rotations at the nodes, all 364, four-way connecting nodes, were unique'. 'After much research, rapid prototyping was found to be the only cost- and time-effective way of producing the nodes' (Elliot, 2001). The complete structure had been modelled digitally, thus all the angles and rotations were known and easily communicated. With assistance from Innovative Manufacture Centre (IMC) at the University of Nottingham ARP was used in conjunction with the lost wax casting process to form the 364 nodes. The rapid prototypes were produced by Multi-Jet Modelling (MJM) and Laminated Object Manufacture (LOM) (see Figure 7.17b). The nodes were optimized by splitting them into bodies and spigots. Conventional tooling techniques were used for the spigots as they were all identical. They were glued into place prior to being used to form the ceramic jackets, of the lost wax casting process (see Chapter 3 for a further description of casting processes). The cast nodes were produced by MBC (see Figure 7.17).

The Integrated Center for Visualization, Design and Manufacture (ICVDM) – University of Waterloo, Ontario

Sited at the Mechanical Engineering Department of the University of Waterloo, Ontario, a centre for visualization, design and manufacture was established during 2001. This centre aims to provide a national centre of excellence serving the global economy. There are four satellite facilities: two on campus at Waterloo in the Department of Computer Science and the School of Architecture, with two off campus at the University of Toronto (Faculty of Architecture, Landscape and Design) and the Laval University (Quebec) School of Architecture. The centre will focus on seamless integration of the virtual and physical world and how this can contribute to the process of design and manufacture. One area of research for the School of Architecture at the University of Waterloo will be the use of rapid prototyping in the building envelope.

Digitizing physical models

Frank Gery has developed a design process which is almost a reverse of rapid prototyping. Starting the design of buildings such as the Guggenheim in Bilbo (see Figure 4.15) by the creation of physical models, sometimes little more than apparently randomly crumpled paper, the design is developed by the production of a series of subtly diverse models. The selected model is then digitized and the digital co-ordinates are used to generate the CAD files. Frank Gery & Associate use Catia, French software originally developed for aerospace applications, which is also widely used in automotive design. The digital data may then undergo an optimization process to produce effective constructional information, such as a steel frame design. Clearly there is great benefit in the design process 'flip flopping' between physical models, sketching and development of design files in a computer.

CAD CAM can be contrasted with the methods used by Sir William Lyons, founder of Jaguar in the design of cars, including the E-Type. A colleague, Bob Knight, describes Sir William Lyons: 'could not draw to save his life; he could only style in metal ... Lyons would walk down to the styling shop and start waving his hands in the air to show what he envisaged. A sheet metalworker would be with him, watching all this, and would set about trying to create what he thought was wanted. It might have been unconventional but it was brilliant and very successful'.[1] In 1948, Jaguar produced the XK120; Bob Knight states that 'Lyons did XK120 in no time: it took only six weeks to design and build the aluminium prototype'.

In 1997, Dr Poselthwaite, the technical director of Tyrell Racing Organisation, committed to a paperless creation of their next Formula One car. He states that

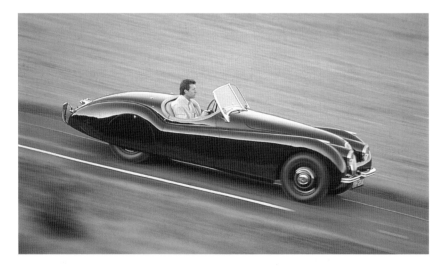

Figure 7.18 Jaguar XK120 (courtesy of *Classic and Sports Car*).

[1]Bob Knight interviewed, *The Times*, 9 May 1998.

Figure 7.19 Photomontage of Ballingdon Bridge for Suffolk County Council (architect Brookes Stacey Randall, engineer Ove Arup & Partners).

'The 1998 chassis was manufactured directly from the 3D CAD geometry. Except for machining purposes, not a single drawing was produced. The CAD data was e-mailed to the machinist, who then used it to create the toolpaths for the CNC machine'. This just-in-time manufacturing process meant that one week before the new car was due to be unveiled to the public 'there was literally nothing in the assembly bay'. However, 'all the parts came together perfectly, the result of being pre-assembled in software and accurately machined from the CAD data' (Poselthwaite, 1999).

The use of CAD files or digital data to directly manufacture components or component tools, alters the relationship between a designer and a manufacturer. The designer has to take direct responsibility for the sizing of a component. The dimension checking process often carried out in the shop drawing's stage, needs to be reintroduced in a new form. The direct exchange of digital data should lead to a stronger partnership between designers and manufacturers: an interdependence born from change, with an immense developmental potential.

Further information

Selected test standards:

AAMA 501.183	Standard test method for curtain walls for water penetration under dynamic pressure
BS 5368	Part 1: 1976=EN42, Air permeability test
	Part 2: 1980=EN86, Weather test under static pressure
	Part 3: 1978=EN77, Wind resistance tests.
BS 476	Fire tests on building materials and structures
BS EN ISO140	Acoustics. Measurement of sound insulation in buildings and building elements
ISO 9705 (1993)	Fire test – full scale room test for surface products
prEN ISO 1182	Reaction to fire tests for building products: non-combustibility test
prEN ISO 1716	Reaction to fire tests for building products: determination of gross calorific value
BS EN ISO 11925	Reaction to fire tests: Ignitability of building products subject to direct impingement of flame
BS EN 12153 (2000)	Curtain Walling. Air permeability. Test method
BS EN 12154 (2000)	Curtain Walling. Watertightness. Performance requirements and classification
BS EN 12155 (2000)	Curtain Walling. Watertightness. Laboratory test under static pressure
BS EN 12179 (2000)	Curtain Walling. Resistance to wind. Test method
prEN 13238	Reaction to fire tests for building products: conditioning procedures and general rules for selection of substrates
prEn 13050	European dynamic weather test.

References

Anon (1999). Fashioning a fast response to change. *Sector Focus the Magazine of the Sector Challenge Programme*, Issue 2, pp. 4–5.

Elliot, G. (2001). (Elliot Wood Partnership), *Architect's Journal*, 12 April, p. 23.

Helweg-Larsen, K. (1985). DD casebook 1 KTAS I Gadebilledet Street Signal. KTAS, p. 76.

Poselthwaite, Dr. H. (1999). CAD, analysis and computer simulation. Development of Tyrell's 1998 F1 car. Time Compression Technologies, Europe, pp. 36–38.

Rice, P. (1994). *An Engineer Imagines*, Artemis, p. 126.

Rotheroe, Dr. K. (2001). Design and Build, *Architects Journal*, 15 March, pp. 46–47.

Suggested reading

Anon, *Guide to Testing and Analysis Services*. RAPRA Technology Ltd.

Fire Spread in Multi-storey Buildings with Glazed Curtain Wall Facades. Loss Prevention Council (Tel. 0208 207 2345).

Porter, T. and Neale, J. (2000). *Architectural Supermodels*, Butterworth-Heinemann

Smith, P. G. and Reinertsen, D. G. (1998). *Developing Products in Half the Time: New Tools, New Rules*. John Wiley & Sons.

Smith, D.A. and Shaw, K. (1999). *European harmonisation of fire test methods – Implications and challenge for manufacturers.* BRE RAPRA Conference Paper.

Stacey, M. (1999). *Digital Design and the Architecture of Brookes Stacey Randall*. Key note address at Arcadia 1998, Arcadia Quarterly.

8

Glossary

AGEING	Precipitation from solid solution resulting in a change in properties of an alloy, usually occurring slowly at room temperature (natural ageing) and more rapidly at elevated temperatures (artificial ageing).
ALLOY	Combination of two or more metals to form enhanced properties.
ANGULARITY	Conformity to, or deviation from, specified angular dimensions in the cross-section of a shape or bar.
ANNEAL	Heating and gradual cooling to modify the properties of a metal, alloy or glass, to attain acceptably low stresses or desired structure or both.
ANODIZING	An electrochemical method of producing an integral oxide film on aluminium surfaces.
ANODIZING QUALITY	Describes material with characteristics that make it suitable for visible anodizing after appropriate preliminary treatment.
AUTOCLAVE	A pressure vessel used for the application of pressure and heat.
BILLET	A cast aluminium product suitable for subsequent extruding. Usually of circular cross-section but may also be rectangular, or elliptical.
BOW	The deviation, in the form of an arc, along the longitudinal axis of a product.
BUFFING	A mechanical finishing operation in which fine

abrasives are applied to a metal surface by rotating fabric wheels for the purpose of developing a lustrous finish.

BURR
A thin ridge of roughness left by a cutting operation such as routing, punching, drilling or sawing.

CIRCUMSCRIBING CIRCLE DIAMETER (CCD)
A circle that will just contain the cross-section of an extrusion, designated by its diameter.

COLD WORK
Plastic deformation of a metal at such a temperature and rate that strain hardening occurs.

COMPOSITE CONSTRUCTION
The combination of materials with very different physically properties to form a single component.

COMPRESSION SET
Defines the degree to which an **elastomer** does not recover fully to its original state after it has been compressed for a long period of time.

CONCAVITY
A concave departure from flat.

CONCENTRICITY
Conformity to a common centre, for example, the inner and outer walls of a round tube.

CONTAINER
A hollow cylinder in an extrusion press from which the billet is extruded.

CONVERSION COATING
Treatment of material with chemical solutions by dipping or spraying to increase the surface adhesion of paint.

COPE
In a split pattern, sand casting the top half of the sand mould or flask is called the cope, whereas the bottom half is the **drag**.

CORE
Lost Wax Casting – an insert in a die to produce an intended void in a pattern. Sand Casting – an insert in the mould to produce an intended void in a casting. Cores can be physically withdrawn, collapsible or dissolvable.

CORROSION
The deterioration of a metal by chemical or electro-chemical reaction with its environment.

CULLET
Broken glass recycled in the glass-making process as a flux, which reduces the melting point and thus energy consumption of the process.

CYLINDER GLASS	Glass produced by blowing a balloon of molten glass, which is rolled in a trough to form a cylinder. The ends are cut off and split down the long side to form a flat rectangular sheet.
DIE	Metal plate, typically steel, with the form to be extruded cut out, through which a material is extruded.
DIE CASTING	Metal casting formed in a metal, typically steel, mould suitable for high volume production.
DIRECT EXTRUSION	A process in which a billet in the container is forced under pressure through an aperture in a stationary die.
DRAG	(When used in a foundry.) In a split pattern, sand casting the bottom half of the sand mould or flask is called the drag, whereas the top half is the **cope**.
DRAFT ANGLE	The taper on the vertical surface of a pattern or mould to permit easy withdrawal of the pattern or product from the mould or die.
DRAWN GLASS	Glass made by a continuous drawing process.
DRAWING	The process of pulling material through a die to reduce the size, or change the cross-section.
DRIFT TEST	A routine sampling test carried out on hollow sections produced by bridge or porthole methods, in which a tapered mandrel is driven into the end of the section until it tears or splits.
ELASTOMER	This is the general term used to describe materials, synthetic or naturally occurring, which have rubbery or elastic properties.
ELECTROLYTIC COLOURING	A two-stage colour **anodizing** process.
ETCHING	The production of a uniform matt finish by controlled chemical (acid or alkali) treatment.
ETCHING TEST	The treatment of a sample using a chemical reagent to reveal the macro-structure of the material.

EXTRUSION RATIO	The ratio of the cross-sectional area of the extrusion container to that of the extruded section (or sections in the case of multi-cavity dies).
FEEDER	Route from the **gate** in a casting mould followed by the molten metal to the mould cavity. Also known as the runner.
FILLET	A concave junction between two surfaces.
FLASK	The boxes which contain the sand used to form a sand casting are called the flask. See **Drag** and **Cope.**
FLOAT GLASS	Glass which has been manufactured by floating the molten glass on a bath of tin at 1100°C; the glass leaves the float tank at about 600°C and passes into the annealing **lehr** where it is cooled to 100°C. This produces a glass with surfaces that are flat and parallel.
FOAMED *IN SITU* PANEL	Composite panel formed by the foaming of the core material, typically polyurethane, which expands to fill the space between and bonds to the skins of the component.
FREE MACHINING ALLOY	An alloy designed to give small broken chips, superior finish and/or longer tool life.
FULL HEAT TREATMENT	Solution treatment followed by artificial ageing.
GATE	End of a **feeder** (or runner) in a casting mould where the molten metal enters the mould.
GRAIN GROWTH	The coarsening of the grain structure of a metal occurring under certain conditions of heating.
GRAIN SIZE	The main size of the grain structure of a metal, usually expressed in terms of the number of grains per unit area or as the mean grain diameter.
HARDNESS	The resistance of a metal to plastic deformation, usually measured by controlled indentation.
HEAT-SOAKING	Toughened glass can be heat soaked at moderately high temperatures following toughening. This acts as a destructive quality control process against the

problem of spontaneous fracture of toughened glass caused by **Nickel Sulphide Inclusions.**

HEAT TOUGHENED GLASS	Glass that has been heated past its softening point and cooled rapidly to create surface compressive stress, which greatly increases strength. It breaks into small fragments if broken. Heat toughened or thermally toughened glass is known in the United States of America as Tempered Glass.
HEAT TREATABLE	An alloy capable of being strengthened by suitable heat treatment.
HEAT STRENGTHENED GLASS	Glass that has been heated past its softening point and chilled rapidly to increase its strength, but breaks like annealed glass.
HOMOGENIZATION	A high temperature soaking treatment to eliminate or reduce segregation by diffusion.
HYSTERESIS	The difference between the amount of energy absorbed when a rubber or **elastomer** is stretched and the amount of energy released when the rubber is relaxed. High hysteresis indicates a high loss of energy (good for energy absorbing applications). Low hysteresis rubbers are more resilient.
INDIRECT EXTRUSION	A process whereby a moving die located at the end of a hollow ram is forced against a stationery billet.
LAMINATION	Bonding together of diverse layers under pressure. Elevated temperature can also be used, typically to reduce curing time.
LEHR	A long, tunnel-shaped oven for heat treating glass by continuous passage.
LOGS	A cast aluminium product suitable for extrusion shipped in full lengths of 7–8 m.
LOST FOAM CASTING	A metal casting formed in a ceramic 'jacket', or investment mould, from which the foam pattern is vaporized by the action of the hot metal as it is cast.

LOST WAX CASTING   A metal casting formed in a ceramic 'jacket', or investment mould, from which the wax pattern has been removed by heating, prior to casting.

MANDREL   Core or former used in filament winding or the extruding of sections.

MEAN DIAMETER   The sum of any two diameters at right angles divided by two.

MEAN WALL THICKNESS   The sum of the wall thickness of a tube measured at the ends of any two diameters at right angles, divided by four.

MECHANICAL PROPERTIES   Those properties of a material that are associated with elastic and inelastic reactions when a force is applied, or that involve the relationship between stress and strain. These properties are often incorrectly referred to as 'physical properties'.

METHOD   The system of **gates, feeders and risers** used to feed a mould cavity to ensure an even distribution of metal with a constant rate of solidification avoiding the formation of unwanted cavities in a casting is called the method.

MIG WELDING   In Metal Inert Gas Welding, a direct current of reverse polarity, is struck between the workpiece and a continuously feed welding rod, which acts as filler and electrode. Penetration cannot be as closely controlled as in TIG Welding.

MONOCOQUE   A structure in which the stiffness is generated by the form of the skins or shell only. Monocoque is literally French for 'single shell'.

NICKEL SULPHIDE INCLUSIONS   Small impurities of nickel sulphide within the glass can 'seed' and expand causing toughened glass to shatter. **Heat-soaking** following toughening acts as a destructive quality control process.

PATTERN   A pattern is a positive of the finished cast component and incorporates the **feeders** and **risers**. It is used to form the mould cavity.

PIT CORROSION	Localized corrosion resulting in small pits in a metal surface.
PLASTICIZER	Liquids that are incorporated into an **elastomer** to create a softening effect.
PLATERN PRESS	Used for laminating, a platen press, comprises a ridge frame within which two ridge and flat plates or platens which can be brought together to provide pressure. Can be heated to reduce cure time.
POLYMER	Organic chemical compound of molecule(s) formed from repeated units or chains of smaller molecules or atoms.
PORTHOLE DIE	An extrusion **die**, also known as a hollow die, that incorporates a **mandrel** as an integral part. Bridge and spider are special forms of this type of **die.** All are used to produce extruded hollow sections from solid **billets.**
PRESS BRAKE	Method of forming sheet metals into profiled linear component(s) using the action of a top and bottom tool, forming the component under pressure.
PULTRUSION	Lineal component, typically incorporating fibre reinforcement that is drawn through a **die**.
QUENCHING	Controlled rapid cooling from an elevated temperature by contact with a liquid, gas or solid.
RAINSCREEN CLADDING	An external cladding that forms an airspace which is drained, bask ventilated, and can be pressure equalized. It protects the inner layers from heavy wetting and solar radiation. Typically the joints are open. The thermal performance and control of permeability are within the inner layer of the wall and do not form part of the rainscreen.
RISER	(When used in a foundry) A reservoir of molten metal provided to compensate for internal contraction of the **casting** as it solidifies.
ROLL FORMING	A method of producing a profiled linear sheet metal component by the progressive development of the shape by roll form tools.

SAND CASTING	A metal casting formed in a sand mould.
SET	When an elastomer is deformed for a long period of time and then released, the degree to which it does not fully recover its original shape is referred to as set; **compression set** or permanent set.
SHORE HARDNESS	Definition of the hardness of an **elastomer** measured in degrees on the Shore 'A' or IRDH scale. (Values are typically similar although Shore 'A' is usually one to three degrees higher).
SOLUTION HEAT TREATMENT	A thermal treatment in which an alloy is heated to a suitable temperature and held for sufficient time to allow soluble constituents to enter into solid solution where they are retained in a supersaturated state after **quenching**.
SPINNING	A flat sheet of the metal is rotated at speed and formed over a hardwood or steel tool. Forming components with a rotated geometry only.
STRAIN	Defines how far the atoms or molecules of a solid material is being pulled part by an external force. $$\text{Strain} = e = \frac{\text{increase in length}}{\text{original length}} = \frac{l}{L}$$
STRESS	This is a measure of how hard the atoms and molecules of a solid material are being pulled apart or pushed together as a result of an external forces. $$\text{Stress} = s = \frac{\text{Load}}{\text{Area}} = \frac{P}{A}$$
SUPERPLASTIC ALLOY	An alloy with high ductility, which is the product of a fine and stabilized grain structure. A superplastic alloy can be capable of elongation of up to 1000%.
TEMPERS	Stable levels of mechanical properties produced in a metal or alloy by mechanical or thermal treatment(s).
THERMOPLASTIC	A material that melts on heating and resets on cooling. This process of melting and re-freezing can

be repeated infinitely. Thus thermoplastics are readily recyclable.

THERMAL RESISTANCE

The measure of resistance to heat flow through a material. Expressed as m °C/W. Thermal conductivity is the inverse W/M °C.

THERMAL TRANSMITTANCE

The property of a building fabric element that describes the steady state heat flow, denoted by the symbol U, hence U-Value. Expressed in W/m^2 °C. It is defined as the quantity of heat that flows in unit time through a unit area of an element when the difference between the temperature of the air on the two sides of the element is 1°.

THERMOSET

A material that melts on heating and then undergoes a permanent change in chemical properties, becoming heat stable. Offers benefits in performance but difficulties in recycling.

TIG WELDING

In Tungsten Inert Arc Welding fusion between the metal components is induced by the arc, which burns between the electrode and the work. This is shielded from the atmosphere by an inert gas such as argon.

TWIST

A winding departure from a flat plane.

ULTIMATE TENSILE STRENGTH

The maximum stress that a material can sustain in tension under a gradual and uniformly applied load.

VACUUM PRESS

Used for laminating; typically a single component is held under pressure by an elastomeric sheet by a partial vacuum created by drawing air through tiny perforations in the steel bed of the press. Also known as Bag Press.

VULCANIZATION

This is the permanent chemical change that a rubber or elastomer undergoes on heating.

YOUNG'S MODULUS

Expresses how stiff or floppy a material is and is designated by E.

Young's Modulus: $E = \dfrac{stress}{strain}$

Index